THE CRIMES OF WATER-GATE

BY FRED J. COOK

A GROLIER COMPANY

FRANKLIN WATTS
New York/London/Toronto/Sydney
1981

Library of Congress Cataloging in Publication Data

Cook, Fred J.
The crimes of Watergate.

Bibliography: p.
Includes index.
Summary: Chronicles the Watergate scandal of 1972
from the break-in to Nixon's resignation and pardon.
1. Watergate Affair, 1972–   —Juvenile literature.
2. Nixon, Richard M. (Richard Milhous), 1913-
—Juvenile literature. [1. Watergate Affair, 1972–   .
2. Nixon, Richard M. (Richard Milhous), 1913–   ]
I. Title.
E860.C68   364.1′32′0973   81–10497
ISBN 0–531–04353–3   AACR2

Photographs courtesy of Wide World Photos:
pp. 83, 84; United Press International: pp. 85, 86, 87, 88,
89, 90, 91, 92.

CONTENTS

THE CRIMES
OF WATERGATE

CHAPTER

1

THE LEGACY
OF WATERGATE

Watergate. The very word has survived as a symbol for political scandal. Watergate. The only scandal ever to force the resignation of an American president.

As the years pass, the name remains buried deep in the consciousness of the American people; the symbol endures with new variations to fit new circumstances. We have had Koreagate, involving the expenditure of vast sums of money by South Korean agents to influence American Congressmen; and, more recently, Billygate—the mysterious $220,000 "loan" to Billy Carter, President Jimmy Carter's brother, by the brutal, anti-Semitic regime of Libya.

So deep and enduring has been the effect of Watergate on the American political process that almost any scandal today becomes some kind of "gate." Yet, as the years pass, the danger grows that the real significance of Watergate will be lost in the glibness of a catchword. Fading memories—and even some propaganda attempts to revise the record—threaten to reduce Watergate to one seemingly irrational, illegal act; one not so very much worse than what had occurred many times before. The record clearly exposes the falseness of such an understanding. Watergate was not just one isolated crime. It was a whole series of crimes that were traced directly to the Oval Office of the White House.

The Watergate scandal broke with barely a whimper at a time when President Richard M. Nixon was riding high in the public-opinion polls, already on his way to the most smashing presidential landslide in American political history. In preparing for the 1972 contest, President Nixon had created, in 1971, a separate political organization—the Committee to Re-Elect the President—soon to become known as CREEP. And it was early on the morning of June 17, 1972, that five undercover agents working for CREEP broke into the headquarters of the Democratic National Committee, located in the posh Watergate apartment-office complex overlooking the Potomac River in downtown Washington, D.C.

The incident seemed vaguely mysterious at the time, although at first most newspapers paid scant attention to it. President Nixon and his aides promptly sought to disclaim any connection with the strange break-in of the rival party's headquarters. Just as desperately, Senator George McGovern, the Democratic candidate for president, and officials of the Democratic party tried to pin responsibility for the break-in on their opponents. Throughout the fall election campaign, the Watergate scandal sputtered under the surface of affairs, with only newspapers such as the *Washington Post* and *The New York Times* paying any attention to it. The American people as a whole seemed unconcerned and voted overwhelmingly for the reelection of President Nixon.

Unparalleled triumph gradually led to unparalleled defeat. There was just too much to cover up. Bit by bit, the stone wall erected by the White House began to crumble, and the American people learned, not just about the Watergate break-in itself, but about a whole series of related crimes.

They learned:

•   That a special undercover squad—in essence, a burglary squad—had been established in the White House itself.

•   This squad had burglarized a psychiatrist's office in California in an attempt to get information to discredit Daniel Ellsberg, a foe of the Vietnam War.

•   The White House agents and the Federal Bureau of Investigation, at White House direction, had indulged in wholesale, illegal wiretapping of lower-echelon government officials and nationally known journalists.

•   Secret agents, financed by CREEP, had infiltrated the Democratic party during the primary period, spreading scurrilous stories that had ruined the campaigns of the stronger Democratic candidates and had assured President Nixon of the weakest possible opponent.

•   President Nixon himself had been involved in a months-long cover-up of Watergate. He had kept the FBI from thoroughly probing the Watergate case. He had encouraged his subordinates to commit perjury and had even advised them on how to do it.

•   He had taped every conversation that took place in the Oval Office, and these tapes, when finally disclosed, showed that he had masterminded the cover-up from the start—and that he had lied, not once but repeatedly, to the American people, to American officials, and even to his own family.

•   The president's language and his unprincipled, unrestrained, vengeful attitude as revealed by the tapes were so coarse and gutter-violent that they shocked almost all who listened.

Watergate is a long and tangled tale that ballooned from what Nixon spokesmen originally called "a third-rate burglary" into "a cancer on the presidency" that brought down the whole administration. Many have attempted to blame Nixon's downfall, as he himself did, on a propaganda campaign against him by the "liberal media." Aside from the fact that the "liberal media" is largely a myth (most large publishers are quite conservative), perhaps the most revealing aspect of the impact of Watergate is to be found in the reactions of many of President Nixon's most conservative and most dedicated followers.

For example, Judge John J. Sirica, who presided over the Watergate trials, had been a lifelong, conservative Republican. He had campaigned for the Eisenhower-Nixon ticket in 1952; he had supported Nixon in 1960 when Nixon lost the presidency to John F. Kennedy; and he had voted for Nixon in 1968 and 1972. He had considered Nixon to be potentially one of our great presidents—until he listened to the tapes.

Judge Sirica, as he wrote in his book, *To Set the Record Straight,* had risen to his position the hard way and was no stranger to the language of the streets. But this hadn't prepared him for what he heard when he listened to the White House tapes. He was appalled by "the barnyard quality of the conversations" and by the discovery that the president had coached his aides on the cover-up. Sirica "found the whole thing disgusting" when he heard the president say: "I want you all to stonewall it, plead the Fifth Amendment, cover up or anything else . . ." After it was all over, Judge Sirica wrote this final judgment of Richard Nixon: "I regret that I supported him in his national campaigns. I hope no political party will ever stoop so low as to embrace the likes of Richard Nixon again."

Equally emphatic was the final judgment of Senator Barry Goldwater of Arizona, the ultraconservative hero of the Republican far right. Goldwater had run for the presidency against Lyndon Johnson in 1964, and Nixon, who had campaigned for him, later fell heir to much of his support. The Goldwater legions, indeed, were largely responsible for the resurrection of Richard Nixon as a presidential candidate in 1968.

During the final days of the Watergate crisis in 1974, Barry Goldwater had been as close to the inner drama as anyone. He had been in the small circle of congressional advisers who had prevailed on Nixon to resign. Yet this stalwart of the right, blunt and outspoken as always, summed up his opinion of Nixon for Harry Reasoner on the CBS *60 Minutes* program of March 9, 1980.

Goldwater said that Nixon "came as close to destroying this country as any one man in that office has ever come," and, "I don't think he should ever be forgiven." "In the last two weeks of the Nixon regime," Goldwater said, "we were teetering on the brink of disaster." He believed that if Nixon had refused to resign and instead risked an impeachment trial in the Senate, the result would have torn the country apart.

Even though Goldwater had campaigned for Nixon—and Nixon for him—he had come to the conclusion that Nixon was a fatally flawed man. "He had a tendency," Goldwater said, "to think first of Richard Milhous Nixon and then think of anybody else and the country. And as I look back on the many things that he did, he was doing them only for himself, and to get himself in that top spot as president. . . . So, he is basically, in my opinion, a dishonest person."

Many (including Judge Sirica) have said that the outcome of Watergate vindicated the American system. It showed that no person, not even the president, is above the law.

It is true that many elements of the system worked as they were supposed to. Judge Sirica, for example, was a stern and conscientious judge; the Senate Watergate Committee, appointed especially to investigate the case, did a thorough job, uncovering new details of the scandal; and the House Judiciary Committee, after studying the evidence, voted to impeach the president.

Still, we were luckier in this case than we have a right to expect if there should be a similar crisis in the future. Judge John Sirica, for example, did not just preside over the trial of the original defendants as many judges would have done. He asked probing questions, virtually taking over the prosecutor's role, an action for which he was criticized by other jurists at the time, but one that was instrumental in breaking the case wide open. The *Washington Post,* almost alone among the American press, followed the story doggedly, in spite of lagging reader interest. And then there were those White House tapes. What would have happened, many asked, if Nixon had not taped his conversations or if he had destroyed them, as many close to him thought he should have done? In either event, the most damaging evidence would have vanished; Nixon almost certainly would have remained in office, and the crimes of Watergate would have remained unexposed. The final verdict, then, would seem to be: yes, the system worked. But it did so only through a combination of fortunate circumstances that might never happen again.

In addition, there are reasons to believe that the Watergate episode played a major role in the increasing disenchantment of the American people with their government. Recent Gallup polls have shown that some 40 to 50 percent of the American people no longer trust their government or believe that it works for them. The record of recent elections reflects this alienation, with only about half of the eligible voters bothering to register and vote.

The decline in voter participation has been steady and steep. In 1960, 63 percent of those eligible cast their ballots; in 1964, 62 percent voted. But by 1976, the figure had dropped to 56.5 percent.

There appear to have been two major causes for dwindling voter interest in the sixties and seventies—Vietnam and Watergate. In 1964, Lyndon Johnson campaigned on a pledge not to send "American boys 8 or 9,000 miles away to do a job that Asian boys ought to be doing for themselves"—all this at the very time he was planning to involve the nation more deeply in Vietnam, the most divisive war in our history. Richard Nixon campaigned in 1968 on a pledge "to bring us together" and to end the war quickly. Instead, he continued it for another four years—and then was exposed in the crimes of Watergate.

One result of this chain of deceit has been the disillusionment of young people. When the voting age was lowered to 18 during the Vietnam War, there were great expectations that a flood of younger voters would effect major political changes in the country. But the outcome showed that the young were so turned off by the system that the great majority did not bother to vote. The U.S. Census Bureau found that, in the 1976 election, only 42.2 percent of the eligibles in the 18–24 age bracket actually voted.

Such figures illustrate a deep disenchantment—a mood indicating that the legacy of Watergate, above all else, may be long-lasting indeed.

CHAPTER 2
THE BREAK-IN

The Watergate complex is a huge, futuristic structure that towers above Virginia Avenue in downtown Washington, D.C. Semicircular in shape, its sawtoothed balustrades rising one above another, it is in reality six buildings—a hotel, two office buildings, and three apartment cooperatives. The view is majestic. Watergate looks out over the Potomac River and down on the Kennedy Center for the Performing Arts. From its high balconies one can look from the Lincoln Memorial eastward across the mall to the Washington Monument, the White House, and the Capitol. During Nixon's first term this swanky complex became known as "the Republican Bastille" because so many high officials nested there and were besieged by Vietnam War protestors.

The Democratic National Committee had rented the entire sixth floor in the office wing of the complex. Ironically, many of their neighbors on the apartment side were persons who were to play prominent roles in the Watergate scandal.

Former Attorney General John N. Mitchell, who had

resigned to head CREEP and direct Nixon's second campaign, was a Watergate resident. So, too, was Maurice H. Stans, former secretary of commerce, in 1972 the finance chairman for the reelection drive. Senator Robert Dole of Kansas, the Republican National Committee chairman, also lived in the Watergate as did Rose Mary Woods, the longtime dedicated private secretary of Richard Nixon.

Such was the elite setting for the political crime of the century.

The Watergate usually had two guards on duty at night, but on the night of June 16–17, 1972, Frank Wills, a young black security guard, was alone. When he made his rounds at 12:45 A.M., he discovered that a door leading from the garage directly into the interior of the office complex had been taped so that the lock would not work and the door could be silently opened by anyone inside wishing to leave in a hurry.

Wills thought that the maintenance men must have taped the lock earlier and forgotten to remove the tapes—so he ripped them off. Then he strolled across the street to have a cup of coffee in the restaurant of the Howard Johnson Motel.

After finishing his coffee, Wills returned to the Watergate and resumed his rounds. When he rechecked the garage, he found to his amazement that the lock on the garage door had again been taped so that it would not work. Obviously, someone who did not belong there must have penetrated into the interior of the Watergate. Wills telephoned the police.

Metropolitan Police Car 727 was cruising only a few blocks from the Watergate when, at 1:52 A.M., Wills' call was relayed to its occupants, Sergeant Paul Leeper and plainclothes officers John Barrett and Carl Schoffler. The three men were members of the so-called "Bum Squad," and their car was unmarked. Since they were all in plain clothes, there was nothing about their attire to indicate that they were police officers. Leeper, for instance, was wearing a golf hat, a light-blue T-shirt, light-blue trousers, and a dark windbreaker imprinted with the words, "George Washington University." Leeper's companions were similarly attired.

As a result, their arrival at the Watergate touched off no alarm bells as well it might have, for the burglars had stationed a lookout on the balcony of the Howard Johnson Motel—a man later identified as Alfred C. Baldwin III, of Connecticut, a former FBI agent. Baldwin was standing on the balcony when he saw Sergeant Leeper and his fellow officers stroll into the Watergate. They looked like any other casually dressed men, and Baldwin dismissed them from his mind.

But not for long. A few minutes later he saw lights flashing back and forth in an office on the eighth floor of the Watergate. The policemen had gone there first because there had been a previous burglary on that floor. Alarmed by the flashing lights, Baldwin grabbed his walkie-talkie. "We've got some activity there," he reported.

"What have you got?" someone called back. Baldwin described the search being made on the eighth floor. "OK, we know about that," a voice he could not identify answered. "That's the two o'clock guard check. Let us know if lights go on any other place."

Sergeant Leeper and the other officers, finding the eighth floor secure, started to work their way down. When they came to the sixth floor, they found that the locks on the doors giving access to the Democratic National Committee's headquarters had been taped. They drew their guns and began a search of the offices, switching lights on and off. Finding nothing, they moved out onto the balcony, flashlights and guns in hand.

Baldwin, seeing three armed men on the balcony, panicked. He realized that the burglary operation was in deep trouble and tried to sound a warning. But he couldn't raise the burglars inside the Watergate. In this most bungled of operations, one of them had turned off their walkie-talkie to save the battery after receiving Baldwin's prior call.

The three policemen, seeing nothing from the balcony, turned back inside and started to penetrate more deeply into the rows of Democratic offices. Soon they spotted a man's arm behind a glass partition. The man was working to insert a bug into the telephone of Lawrence F. O'Brien, chairman of the Democratic National Committee.

"Hold it!" one of the policemen shouted. "Stop! Come out!"

The officers were astounded when, suddenly, not two arms but ten were raised up into the air.

"Are you gentlemen the metropolitan police?" inquired the man who had been bugging O'Brien's phone.

Informed that they were indeed confronting policemen, the five burglars surrendered quietly. Theirs was to be about the last quiet act in the Watergate drama, but few appreciated this at the time. The news of the arrests could hardly be said to have burst upon the American scene like a bombshell. *The New York Times*, in its Sunday, June 18, edition reported this mysterious little occurrence under a four-column headline: "Five Charged With Burglary at Democratic Headquarters." The headline and story appeared at the bottom of page 30, buried under news that seemed, at the time, more significant.

CHAPTER 3
THE FIRST CLUES

The arrested men were all taken to the Second District Police Station, where it soon became obvious that these were no ordinary burglars. When arrested, all of the men had been wearing blue Playtex surgical gloves. They also had with them an extraordinary amount of spying equipment: a walkie-talkie, forty rolls of unexposed film, two 35-mm cameras, lock picks, pen-sized tear-gas guns, and bugging devices capable of picking up not only telephone conversations but anything said in the room in which the bugged phone was located.

Even more peculiar, and later to prove more important to the investigation that would follow, was the fact that these were exceptionally well-heeled burglars. Searching their captives, detectives found that they had in their pockets a total of $1,300. Even stranger was the fact that all of the money was in consecutively numbered $100 bills.

This was only the beginning. Examining the Watergate Hotel register, detectives learned that on June 16 the five men had checked into rooms 214 and 314. Examination of the rooms turned up another $3,200 in neat packages of $100 bills, again all consecutively numbered.

There were other clues. In the pocket of one suspect, later identified as Bernard Barker, detectives found a check made out to the Lakewood Country Club and signed by someone named E. Howard Hunt. They also found an address book with the initials H.H. in it. And there was a telephone number beside the initials, with the notation "W. House."

When first questioned at the police station, all of the burglars gave false names. The man who had been spotted in the act of bugging Lawrence O'Brien's phone said he was "Ed Martin."

These very suspicious details were phoned into the *Washington Post* by Alfred E. Lewis, a police reporter for thirty-five years whose deeds had become a legend among Washington newsmen. Under the impact of these unfolding discoveries, wheels at the *Post* began to turn. Harry Rosenfeld, the metropolitan editor, telephoned the *Post's* publisher, Katharine Graham, and told her: "You will not believe what is going on."

Then Rosenfeld called in Barry Sussman, his District of Columbia editor, who began to round up his forces. Bob Woodward, who with his partner, Carl Bernstein, was later to write the bestseller *All the President's Men,* was asleep in his apartment at nine o'clock that Saturday morning when his jangling phone woke him. Sussman told Woodward about the break-in and ordered him to report to the newspaper office at once.

The five arrested men, Woodward learned, were to be arraigned in metropolitan court that afternoon. He went to cover the hearing. It was 3:30 P.M. when all five, dressed in conservative business suits, were led before Judge James A. Belsen. The judge asked the men their professions. One spoke up and said they were "anti-Communists." Obviously, something more was needed.

The tallest of the suspects finally stepped forward. He

had shed the phony name of "Ed Martin" and given his true name—James W. McCord, Jr. He was a sturdily built man, balding, with strands of black hair combed straight back over his scalp. He had a rugged face, with a strong chin and deep creases in his cheeks that looked as if they might have been caused by a habit of keeping his jaw firmly clamped and his cheeks sucked in.

When Judge Belsen asked his occupation, McCord replied, "Security consultant."

McCord said he had recently retired from government service and set up his own security business.

"Where in government?" Judge Belsen asked.

"CIA," said McCord in a voice barely above a whisper.

The judge was startled. Young Bob Woodward almost fell off his seat. The Central Intelligence Agency is the nation's number one spy organization, and here was one of its former agents caught illegally entering the Watergate!

The CIA angle became more intriguing before the day was out, as Woodward's collaborator, Carl Bernstein, checked the identities of the four men arrested along with McCord. All were from Miami—and all, in one way or another, had CIA connections.

Bernard Barker, in whose coat detectives had found that mysterious check signed by a certain E. Howard Hunt, was known in the Cuban community as a fanatical anti-Communist. He had been a leader in the Cuban Brigade that had tried unsuccessfully to overthrow Fidel Castro in the disastrous Bay of Pigs invasion of 1961, and later he had participated in CIA-sponsored activities against the Castro regime.

Two of the other arrested burglars were also Cubans, also known to have been involved in anti-Castro activities and to have had connections with the CIA. Virgilio R. Gonzalez was a skilled locksmith—the reason he had been recruited for the Watergate job. He was the man who had picked the lock on the garage door to gain access to the interior of the Watergate complex. Eugenio R. Martinez, like

Barker and Gonzalez, had been engaged in anti-Castro plots and was still, as it later developed, on the payroll of the CIA.

The last of the four was the only other American. He was a swashbuckling soldier-of-fortune named Frank A. Sturgis, also known as Frank Fiorini. Sturgis had been a Castro aide; he had later split with the dictator and become a violent anti-Castroite, aiding the CIA in several of its futile plots to assassinate the Cuban dictator.

From the outset, these ties lifted the Watergate burglary far above the status of "a third-rate burglary," the level at which Nixon spokesmen tried to keep it. The use of an undercover squad of men who had been so closely connected with the CIA gave the affair, from the start, a suspiciously official taint. But many questions remained to be answered.

Who was E. Howard Hunt? What were his connections? What role did he play?

What was the story behind James McCord, the former CIA agent now in the "security business?" What kind of "security agent" becomes a burglar?

And, finally, what about that hoard of $100 bills? Not just ordinary $100 bills but bills numbered in exact sequence, as if they had all come from one central source. What source? That was the crucial question.

CHAPTER
4
AT THE DOOR
OF CREEP

The answers to all the nagging questions existed in a building across the street from the White House complex—the offices of **CREEP**, at 1701 Pennsylvania Avenue N.W.

Traditionally, presidential campaigns have been run through the apparatus provided by a party's national committee. The chairman of the national committee is the party spokesperson and is in charge of grass-roots organizations. The national committee incurs the campaign debts and raises the funds, milking the "fat cats" who hope to gain influence with a candidate and organizing those expensive testimonial dinners to pay off past debts or amass a treasure chest for the new endeavor.

Richard Nixon chose not to use the traditional system. He bypassed the national party organization. In April 1971, he created the Committee to Re-Elect the President, all of whose fund-raising and other activities were to be devoted to the interests of one man—Richard M. Nixon.

Ruling over CREEP, at first from the respectful distance of the attorney general's office, was tough, law-and-order John Mitchell. Mitchell and Nixon had become friends after Nixon shook the dirt of California from his feet following his defeat by incumbent Governor Edmund (Pat) Brown in the gubernatorial contest of 1962. Mitchell and Nixon occupied adjoining offices in the law firm of Nixon, Mudge, Rose, Guthrie, and Alexander in New York, and Nixon soon acquired a deep respect for Mitchell, one of the most astute bond lawyers in the nation.

Bald, long-visaged, dour-faced Mitchell was a quiet man who almost invariably had a pipe stuck in his mouth. At a conference table he would sit quietly smoking his pipe, until everyone else had spoken. Then he would give his opinion, usually with tart, blunt good sense. He so impressed Nixon that, when Nixon's political fortunes showed signs of reviving in the primary season of 1968, Nixon enticed Mitchell from the bond business and placed him in charge of organizing his campaign staff.

Gearing up for 1972, Nixon again turned to Mitchell. He didn't want to lose Mitchell's services as attorney general right away, so he asked Mitchell to set up a staff that could run CREEP until later in the campaign, when Mitchell himself would resign as attorney general and take control of CREEP.

This led to the appointment of, as deputy director in charge of CREEP, a slick young hustler on the way up— Jeb Stuart Magruder. Magruder was 36, smart, and handsome. He had been a salesman and merchandise manager before he got into politics. Moving from job to job, he wound up as a $30,000-a-year cosmetics buyer for a California chain.

Magruder had worked in the Nixon campaigns of 1960 and 1962; in 1968 he was an organizer for Nixon in southern California. There he caught the eye of H.R. (Bob) Haldeman, who was later to become Nixon's chief of staff in the White House. Haldeman, always on the lookout for young, aggressive, conservative types, brought Magruder to Washington.

Magruder's talent for writing clear, concise memoranda that conveyed the impression he had a firm grasp of details had impressed both Haldeman and Mitchell. And so when a surrogate commander was needed to run CREEP until Mitchell would take over, Jeb Magruder was tabbed for the $38,500-a-year job, complete with a chauffeured limousine. He took with him to CREEP two other ambitious young men, Hugh W. Sloan, Jr., who was to serve as treasurer of the committee, and Robert Odle, Jr., the office manager.

CREEP immediately became the center for activities unlike any that had ever before taken place in American politics. In a secret "war room" inside CREEP offices, Magruder put on display a sign that read:

"WINNING IN POLITICS
ISN'T EVERYTHING;
IT'S THE ONLY THING."

The motto fitted perfectly the style of the man who was to serve under Magruder as "the intelligence chief" of CREEP. This was G. Gordon Liddy, a man with an erect military bearing, black hair receding from a high forehead, and a black moustache above a firmly set mouth. Liddy was a man with fanatical tendencies. On more than one occasion he expressed the belief that Jack Anderson, the Washington columnist whose ability to get inside information often put burrs under the seats of presidents, should be assassinated. In 1968, when running for Congress in New York's wealthy Westchester County, Liddy would often climax his public speeches by stripping off his jacket and tapping on a revolver he kept in a shoulder holster, implying that the gun was his answer to everything.

Such was the man who directed the Watergate break-in, assisted by another sleuth from the Nixon underground, E. Howard Hunt—the person whose name was on Barker's check and whose White House telephone number was in the address book found in the hotel. Hunt had had a long spy career, first in World War II and later with the CIA. He had been one of the CIA's top consultants in planning the Bay of Pigs invasion and so had developed contacts with Cuban anti-Castroites in Miami. They knew him as "Eduardo" and believed that he had important connections at the highest levels of American government.

The Liddy-Hunt team, with their Cuban associates, had actually burglarized the Democratic National Committee headquarters once before, on Memorial Day weekend, some three weeks before their final unsuccessful attempt. They had bugged the telephone of R. Spencer Oliver, a Democratic liaison with fund-raisers, and they had attempted to bug the phone of Lawrence O'Brien.

The bug on Oliver's phone had worked just fine, producing no vital information but some interesting chitchat. This was picked up on a receiving set by Alfred Baldwin in his room at the Howard Johnson Motel. Baldwin made verbatim copies of the conversations, typed them up, and sent them to CREEP. Copies were kept in a Liddy file marked "Gemstone," and retyped versions were sent on to the White House.

It was the failure of the O'Brien bug to work properly that led Liddy and Hunt to decide on the second, June 17, break-in. As in the first attempt, the services of James McCord, a veteran CIA bugging expert, were enlisted.

The arrest of the five burglars during this second foray touched off several waves of panic. Hunt and Liddy had been waiting in one of the rented Watergate rooms, 214, for their burglary squad to return and tell them, "Mission accomplished." When Baldwin saw the police on the balcony and failed to contact the burglars, he then radioed Hunt: "Base One to Unit One. Are our people dressed in suits or dressed casually?"

"Our people are dressed in suits," Hunt replied.

"Well, we've got problems," Baldwin told him. "We've got some people dressed casually, and they've got guns . . ."

Hunt became "absolutely panic-stricken" at this news, Baldwin later said. He tried to warn the burglars, failed, and called back to Baldwin, "Stay there; I'll be right over."

Baldwin saw Hunt and Liddy leave the Watergate, climb into their car and drive around the block. "You better not park near this building," he warned them. "Police are all over the block."

"OK," Hunt replied.

Soon afterward, Hunt dashed into Baldwin's motel room, took one look out the window at the milling police scene below, then fled into the bathroom. Emerging a few moments later, he grabbed a bedside phone and dialed a local number. "I've got to call a lawyer," he explained to Baldwin. "They've had it."

After he made the call, Hunt turned to Baldwin and asked, "Do you know where McCord lives?" Baldwin said he did. Hunt then pointed to the electronic equipment that littered the room. McCord's wallet, car keys, and loose change were also lying on the bed.

"Well, get all that stuff out of here," Hunt ordered. "And you get out of here, too."

With that, Hunt unhooked his walkie-talkie, threw it on the bed, and rushed out of the room. Baldwin did as he had been ordered. He cleaned out the room, drove to McCord's home in Virginia, left all the incriminating evidence with McCord's wife, and then headed home to Connecticut.

The panic at the Watergate scene was only the first wave of frenzy to sweep the Nixon administration. At CREEP headquarters Robert Odle, the office manager, heard about the Watergate break-in, but at first didn't know any of the details. His reaction was one of relief.

"That could never happen here," he told another CREEP employee, "because I have this guy working for me named Jim McCord, and he has got this place really tight, and all I can say is, I'm glad McCord works for me."

Minutes later, Odle got a telephone call. It was from Mrs. McCord, saying that her husband was in jail and needed a lawyer.

Odle hadn't yet recovered from this shock when a disheveled G. Gordon Liddy burst upon the scene. He encountered Hugh Sloan, CREEP's treasurer, and blurted out,

"My boys got caught last night. I made a mistake. I used somebody from here, which I told them I would never do. I'm afraid I'm going to lose my job."

Next, Liddy encountered Odle in the corridor.

"Where is the office shredding machine?" he asked.

Odle told him it was on the second floor. Liddy vanished into his office and moments later reemerged, carrying a foot-high stack of papers. He headed in the direction of the shredder. Seconds later he was back, demanding, "How do you work this thing?"

Shown how the shredder worked, Liddy closed the door and began to feed his files into it. He then added every consecutively numbered $100 bill he possessed and all the paper soap-wrappers he had collected from every hotel he had visited. The cover-up was as complete as he could make it. But in the long run it wouldn't do him any good.

Too many persons were involved, too many knew. And the panic and cover-up at CREEP were only the fore-runners of the greater panic and cover-up on the higher levels of the Nixon administration.

CHAPTER
5
THE FIRST FALLOUT

The president and "the president's men," as Woodward and Bernstein were to call them, were scattered all across the nation on that fateful Saturday morning when the Watergate bombshell burst.

Richard Nixon, whose diplomatic triumphs included the resumption of relations with Communist China and a détente with Soviet Russia, had just returned from one of his foreign missions. Riding the crest of his achievements in foreign affairs, he had gone to his private retreat in Key Biscayne, Florida, for a rest. With him were Haldeman, the martinet who was his chief of staff, and Ronald Ziegler, the White House press secretary.

Another member of the White House hierarchy close to the president was back in Washington. This was John Ehrlichman, the president's domestic adviser and Haldeman's partner in blocking access to Nixon and erecting around him what became known to friends and foes alike as "the Berlin Wall."

A young man named John W. Dean III, who was to play a pivotal role in the unfolding drama, was on a mission to the Philippines. Virtually unknown to the press and public at the time, Dean held the title of counsel to the president. He was soon to be enmeshed in plans to contain the Watergate fallout and cover up any White House connection to the break-in.

A large contingent of the Nixon team was in California. Taft Schreiber, vice-president of MCA, a huge entertainment conglomerate, was hosting a big Hollywood fund-raising party for the Nixon campaign that Saturday night. It had been obligatory, therefore, for the stars of the Nixon political show to be present so they could be gazed upon by the stars of Hollywood.

John Mitchell, who had left the attorney general's office in February 1972 to assume active command of CREEP, headed the delegation. Magruder was with him. So was Frederick C. LaRue, a wealthy Mississippi oilman, a Republican pioneer in Southern politics, and Mitchell's close associate in CREEP. Another member of the group was Robert Mardian, who had served under Mitchell as an assistant attorney general in charge of a nationwide campaign to ferret out "subversives" among opponents of the Vietnam War.

This congenial group, soon to be conspirators all, were having breakfast in the fashionable Polo Lounge of the Beverly Hills Hotel when a telephone call came for Jeb Magruder. Gordon Liddy was on the line.

"Can you get to a secure phone?" Liddy asked.

"No," said Magruder. "What's the matter?"

"There has been a problem."

"What kind of a problem?"

"Our security chief has been arrested in the Watergate."

"Do you mean Jim McCord?"

"Yes."

Magruder was stunned. He walked back to the breakfast table and whispered the shocking news to LaRue. "You know," he said, "I think last night was the night they were going into the DNC." LaRue advised him to find a pay phone and call Liddy back. Magruder did, but there was not much more that Liddy could tell him beyond the fact that McCord and four others had been arrested as they were trying to bug Larry O'Brien's phone.

LaRue then broke the news to Mitchell. "This is incredible," Mitchell said.

Mitchell, Magruder, and Mardian consulted together. They decided to try for the quick fix. Richard Kleindienst, an old-time Barry Goldwater supporter, had been Mitchell's assistant in the Justice Department and had succeeded Mitchell as attorney general. The conspirators around the breakfast table decided to telephone Liddy and tell him to get Kleindienst to spring McCord, CREEP's man, from the Washington jail.

Kleindienst was having an early lunch at the Burning Tree Country Club when Liddy tracked him down. Liddy asked him to free McCord, telling him that John Mitchell had requested it. Kleindienst refused. Liddy pleaded. He told Kleindienst that he was afraid some of the men arrested in the Watergate might be connected either with the White House or CREEP.

At this point Kleindienst, who had no use for Liddy, practically ran him off the premises. But beyond this he did not go. He must have suspected from what Liddy had told him that Liddy himself was deeply involved in Watergate, either as a participant in the crime or as one who had guilty knowledge of it. But Kleindienst kept this information to himself. He did not notify the FBI, and it was twelve days before FBI agents stumbled upon the existence of Gordon Liddy.

The refusal of Kleindienst to go along with the quick police-court fix killed the easy cover-up at birth. It meant that the cover-up—and everyone assumed, as Magruder later testified, that naturally there would have to be a cover-up —would be a longer, much more difficult, and much trickier process. In the meantime, since the national press wires were carrying the Watergate story, it became necessary for presidential spokesmen to say *something*.

John Mitchell was elected for the task. On Sunday, responding to a query from the Associated Press, he issued a statement that had little connection with the truth. After referring to McCord's arrest, he said:

"The person involved is the proprietor of a private security agency who was employed by our committee months ago to assist with the installation of our security system. He has, as we understand it, a number of business clients and interests, and we have no knowledge of those relationships.

"We want to emphasize that this man and the other people involved were not operating either on our behalf or with our consent.

"I am surprised and dismayed at these reports . . .

"There is no place in our campaign or in the electoral process for this type of activity, and we will not permit or condone it."

It is a statement to bear in mind, not only in the light of what had already happened, but in the light of all that was to follow.

This was the situation when John Dean, flying in from the Far East, stepped off his plane in California that same Sunday morning, June 18. Dean telephoned his assistant in Washington, Fred Fielding. Fielding broke the news to him and urged him to hurry back to Washington because there might be problems to be handled.

"I was more appalled than surprised," Dean later testified. "I can't say I anticipated it," he explained, "but I can't say I was surprised to hear of it because I was aware of the fact that a past effort had been made to accomplish a burglary on the Brookings Institute [Institution] and I had also heard of the Ellsberg psychiatrist break-in by that time."

The atmosphere of the Nixon White House, then, was such that burglaries and evil tricks of every sort were standard operating procedure. And so John Dean was not "surprised" by what had happened at the Watergate; he was only "appalled" that the burglars had been arrested—and what this implied for the road ahead.

CHAPTER
6
"THAT ZOO UP THE STREET"

President Nixon was the man who presided over what even Richard Kleindienst called "that zoo up the street." Neither John Mitchell nor Kleindienst had wanted Dean, a brilliant young hand in the Justice Department, to accept the White House appointment when it was offered to him. Both had warned him against pitfalls in the super-charged atmosphere of the White House, and Kleindienst had referred to it often in less than respectful terms.

No understanding of the series of crimes represented by Watergate is possible without some understanding of the personality of Richard Nixon. Most sources agree that he was, in essence, two men.

Though he had overcome seemingly insurmountable odds to sit in the White House, Richard Nixon was basically an insecure man. Born poor in Yorba Linda, California, he had had to fight and scramble his way up. Others have faced the same problems but been able to overcome the original insecurities linked to them. Nixon could not. He was always a man in desperate struggle. He was a man who often felt that the whole world was against him—and so he lashed out viciously and vindictively against the host of his imagined enemies. He recognized no rules of fair play. He fought with no holds barred.

Theodore H. White, who has made a profession of chronicling American presidential campaigns, tried after Watergate to solve the riddle of Nixon's personality. He interviewed the white-haired lady who had been the debating coach at Whittier High School. She remembered Nixon's good qualities: he had ability, he was smart, he worked hard. But she had never liked him. She had found, White wrote, "something mean in him . . . mean in the way he put his questions, argued his points."

White questioned Pat Buchanan, a Nixon loyalist and speechwriter, and asked him, "What went wrong?" Buchanan, almost in agony, burst out, "It runs to the president himself. There's a mean side to his nature you've never seen—I can't talk about it." John Ehrlichman phrased it this way: "There was another side to him, like the flat, dark side of the moon."

David Frost, in his extensive research for the television interview series he did with Nixon, encountered the same dual personality. One domestic political adviser, Frost wrote, "theorized that there were really two Nixons: the one who was fascinated with both great international issues and the mechanics of governing, and the frighteningly insecure political thug."

The political thug had dominated most of Nixon's career, and Watergate can perhaps best be understood by looking more closely at this aspect of his character. The "meanness" that his high school debating teacher had spotted in him erupted when he took to the campaign trail. When he first ran for Congress in 1946, his opponent was the Democratic incumbent, Jerry Voorhis, a moderate liberal and an on-the-record foe of communism. Voorhis had compiled a good record in Congress, but Nixon smeared him "Red" in what became known as "the pink sheet" campaign. Certain of Voorhis' votes on national issues were displayed on pink-dyed fliers, and Voorhis was destroyed politically. "For vicious irresponsibility there were few campaigns like Nixon's first attack on Voorhis," White later wrote.

Reelected in 1948, Nixon sprang into national prominence as the man who exposed Alger Hiss, a State Department official in the Roosevelt and Truman administrations, who had been accused of Communist ties and passing information to a Communist spy courier. Riding the crest of headline publicity, Nixon campaigned in 1950 to unseat Senator Helen Gahagan Douglas—and "the political thug" emerged again. The same "pink sheet" tactic was used in an unprincipled campaign "surpassing even his slander of Voorhis," White wrote.

Throughout his political career, Nixon used the same tactics of tarnishing political opponents by calling into question not their ability but their patriotism. Secretary of State Dean Acheson was a hard-liner where communism was concerned, but Nixon denounced his "Kollege of Komunism, Kowardice and Korruption." President Harry S. Truman, one of the most admired of our modern presidents, was savaged by Nixon for running an administration of "K1-C3, Korea, Communism, Corruption, and Controls."

These gutter-fighter instincts of Nixon's meshed perfectly with the newly emerging style of unprincipled political campaigning that had gotten its start in California. Public relations firms such as Whittaker and Baxter and Spencer-Roberts were among the first to use the "attack" campaign. A political opponent must be fought like an enemy in war. He or she must be remorselessly attacked. Issues must be kept simple and clear; they must be made emotional. If an "enemy" doesn't exist to arouse this kind of emotion, invent one. In the 1940s and 1950s, with the advent of the Cold War and the threat of Russian imperialism, anti-communism was a tailor-made issue for this kind of emotional campaign. All an unprincipled candidate had to do, regardless of facts, was to smear an opponent with a broad "Red" brush.

This public relations technique made Richard Nixon

in the beginning, and throughout his political career he used public relations to make and remake his image. When he ran for higher office and had to abandon the tactics of "the political thug," it was public relations that presented the electorate with a "new Nixon."

Watergate brings together two facts of Nixon's life: his basic insecurity, intensified by several severe political defeats that drove him to extremes to ensure victory; and public relations, which became for him the magic solution to all of his problems. Throughout the Watergate turmoil, one finds the president and his closest advisers talking only about "taking the PR route," about "managing" the disclosures, about adopting "a modified limited hang-out," and so on.

The public relations gimmickry designed to blur or distort truth came naturally to these men; it had been their life and training. None except Nixon came to Washington with any experience in national politics or government; they just came convinced that they could "PR" and "manage" everything. A quick rundown of those closest to the Oval Office and most influential in the cover-up reveals something of the kind of people welcomed in the Nixon White House:

•   Henry Robbins Haldeman, the chief of staff, had been the West Coast head of the J. Walter Thompson advertising agency, hawking the virtues of Seven-Up, Sani-Flush, and Black Flag insecticide.

•   John D. Ehrlichman had been a classmate of Haldeman's at the University of California at Los Angeles; he had engaged, with Haldeman, in right-wing campus politics and then had become a lawyer, specializing in real estate and insurance in Seattle.

•   Ronald L. Ziegler, the White House press secretary, was another ex-employee of the J. Walter Thompson agency, having worked with Haldeman on the Disneyworld account.

•   Dwight L. Chapin, the White House appointments secretary, a position of key access to the president, was another protegé of Haldeman's from J. Walter Thompson's.

•   Jeb Stuart Magruder had been a merchandiser, a specialist in cosmetics.

•   John N. Mitchell, a bond lawyer, had amazed Nixon by his ability to pick up a telephone, call the right contact, and get a bond upgraded.

Manipulators all, their skills lay in trying to turn night into day, black into white; and their expertise matched the desires of the man in the Oval Office who, throughout his public life, had relied on PR techniques to make or modify his image. PR, then, would be used to whitewash Watergate.

But why did Watergate occur in the first place? The Democrats were in complete disarray in the summer of 1972. Every public opinion poll showed that President Nixon had an overwhelming lead over Senator George McGovern. So where was the need for Watergate?

The answer is traceable, most sources agree, to the basic insecurity at the core of Nixon's personality. He was not an outgoing, gregarious, natural politician; even the V-for-Victory wave of his uplifted arms seemed somehow mechanical and forced, his smile tight and unspontaneous. He was a man who had climbed the heights despite these handicaps, but the climb had been beset with severe and humiliating setbacks and a final wafer-thin victory that had done nothing to enhance his confidence.

Vice-president for two terms in the administration of Dwight D. Eisenhower, Nixon was the Republican presidential candidate in 1960. He began with a sizable lead in the polls over Senator John F. Kennedy, but Kennedy defeated him by the narrowest of margins. In 1962 he returned to his native California and attempted to rebuild his political base in a campaign against Governor Brown.

This time he was repudiated by the voters in his own state and beaten decisively.

On that election night, as the magnitude of his defeat became clear, Nixon lost all control of himself. Television screens across the nation recorded the astonishing scene. Herbert Klein, Nixon's press spokesman, was delivering Nixon's statement conceding defeat to a crowd of newspaper and television reporters. Suddenly, Nixon appeared behind Klein, rushed to the platform, shoved Klein aside, and seized the microphone. "He looked his worst," Jules Witcover later wrote in *The Resurrection of Richard Nixon*. "The small, dark eyes, tight mouth, rubbery nose and self-conscious demeanor that had made Nixon the cartoonists' delight presented him at his least photogenic."

Nixon launched into a long, rambling, and at times almost incoherent monologue. He had always blamed a partisan press, believing it his enemy and forgetting that, in the days of the Hiss case, that same press had made him look heroic. Going back and forth in his tirade, he first denounced the press then drew back, saying that the press had only been doing its job—then lashed out again as his anger overwhelmed him. Reporters sat stunned by the spectacle. Near the end, it seemed, Nixon wrote his own obituary with these bitter words:

"But as I leave you I want you to know—just think how much you're going to be missing. You won't have Nixon to kick around any more because, gentlemen, this is my last press conference. . . ."

It is doubtful that there was a political reporter in America who believed after that incredible scene that Richard Nixon could stage a political comeback. But he did.

The times, of course, played into his hands. President Kennedy was assassinated in Dallas, Texas, on November 22, 1963, and Lyndon Johnson became president. Johnson, one of the most powerfully persuasive men ever to sit in the White House, had hardly taken office when he made the determination not to "lose Vietnam" the way President

Truman had been accused by Nixon and others of "losing China." That decision was to plunge the nation into the most divisive war in our history—a war that cost more than 300,000 American casualties and ended in defeat.

Violent opposition to this faraway war, which most Americans came to consider none of their business, forced President Johnson to withdraw from the 1968 race. He endorsed Vice-president Hubert H. Humphrey to succeed him, but Humphrey had been such a vociferous supporter of the Vietnam War that anti-war protestors descended upon the Democratic National Convention in Chicago. The result was violent street rioting such as Americans had never before seen at a national convention. Humphrey won the nomination, but came out of the convention at the head of a party that had literally torn itself apart.

Nixon, in the meantime, had inherited the Goldwater legions now recovering from their 1964 debacle, had collected a political lifetime of I.O.U.'s, and had become the Republican presidential candidate. Considering the internal war among the Democrats, it seemed impossible that he could lose. But he almost did.

Humphrey, a whirlwind campaigner, nearly closed the gap, and Governor George Wallace, of Alabama, carried five Southern states. The result was that Nixon, though victorious, took office as a minority president, elected by only 43.6 percent of the national vote, the smallest percentage since Woodrow Wilson's 41.9 percent in 1912.

Given the basic insecurities of Richard Nixon, given this succession of defeats and final wafer-thin victory, given his "attack" philosophy that knew no scruples in the uphill scramble to win, it is easy to see how the seeds of Watergate germinated. The man who had lost when he should have won, and who had won by only a hair when he should have triumphed, was just the kind of man to throw all his resources into winning big in 1972 and into making certain that nothing would go wrong this time.

CHAPTER
7
THE PLUMBERS

Richard Nixon had hardly taken the oath of office before he began the first of a series of steps that were to lead ultimately to the crimes of Watergate.

Fund-raising affairs were held in 1969 and 1970 "to pay off the 1968 campaign debts." What most Republican leaders themselves didn't know was that there was no debt. The Nixon forces had done a lot of secret fund-raising outside the normal channels of the party. Herbert Kalmbach, Nixon's personal attorney in California, had raised $6 million; and after the 1968 campaign was over, he had custody of the $2 million that hadn't been spent.

Only four weeks after he took office, Nixon set in motion another secret fund-raising drive. He planned to use these funds to help put together a conservative coalition from the people his propagandists had dubbed "the Silent Majority."

The development of such a coalition depended on what became known as "the Southern strategy." The states of the deep South had resisted integration for centuries, and demagogic appeals with racist overtones still pulled a lot of voters into the polling booths. The champion of the seg-regationist South was George Wallace. Nixon and his advisers felt, no doubt correctly, that the five states Wallace had carried in 1968 would have voted for Nixon if Wallace had not been in the race. The solution, then, was to eliminate Wallace as a threat in the 1972 campaign.

In 1970 Wallace was locked in a bitter fight with Albert P. Brewer for the Democratic gubernatorial nomination. Obviously, if Wallace could be defeated he would be discredited in his own state and finished as a national candidate. And so, to achieve this end, some $400,000 were taken out of the secret Kalmbach fund and sent to Alabama to support Brewer's campaign. Brewer won the primary but failed to get the necessary majority of votes. In the subsequent runoff, Wallace defeated him by a narrow margin of three percentage points.

What was significant about this first dubious use of the secret fund was that it set a precedent for much that was to follow. Although there was nothing illegal about supporting Brewer with $400,000, the Nixon forces had taken a virtually unprecedented step by trying to influence the primary process of the opposition party. It was a tactic that, carried to extremes—as it soon was—could threaten the very basis of the two-party system.

Presidential campaigns have always had their seamy side. Each party tries to spy on the other, attempting to get advance information of the opposition's campaign plans and position papers. But this kind of back-and-forth sniping usually takes place *after* the major parties have selected their candidates. What Nixon was doing was something entirely different and more insidious; he was tampering with the very selection process of his opposition, using vast secret funds to prevent the free choice of his rival. The anti-Wallace effort was just the first in a series of disruptive actions that destroyed the strongest Democratic candidates of 1972 and left Nixon with just what he wanted—the weakest possible opponent.

To achieve such ends, recruits were needed; and between presidential staffing powers and Kalmbach's secret fund, they were not hard to find. One who joined the White House's own "dirty tricks" brigade in November 1969 was a stockily built, round-faced, bespectacled native of Massachusetts, Charles (Chuck) Colson. Though he came from one of the most liberal states in the Northeast, Colson's policies were as far right as any of those in the California brigade. Republicans, Colson felt, were a trampled-upon minority in Massachusetts, and Colson was filled with such bitter resentment against the so-called Harvard Liberal Establishment that he was willing to go to any extreme in the underground political war to see his views prevail.

One quote is enough to show the nature of the man. "I would walk over my grandmother if necessary [for Richard Nixon]," he said. No wonder Chuck Colson became known as the hatchetman of the White House.

The Nixon administration was only two months old when John Ehrlichman, from his office on the second floor of the West Wing, just above the Oval Office, set about developing "investigative support for the White House." It might seem that the White House, with the U.S. Department of Justice and the FBI at its command, had all the legitimate investigative support it would need. But Nixon wanted his own cloak-and-dagger operation, responsible only to him and free from the customary restraints of the law.

And so it happened that two former New York detectives joined the Nixon underground. The first was Jack Caulfield, a second-grade detective who had been assigned as liaison to Nixon's campaign headquarters during the 1968 election. He joined the White House staff on April 8, 1969. Obviously, he needed an assistant, and he recommended a friend, Tony Ulasewicz, for the job. In June Ulasewicz was hired with the understanding that he was not to go near the White House but was to receive his orders from Caulfield. Ulasewicz was to be paid out of the Kalmbach fund at a rate of $22,000 a year (later raised to $24,000) and $1,000 a month expenses.

Such was the beginning. Once started, there was to be virtually no limit to the expansion and activities of Nixon's own secret band of operatives. And it was opposition to the Vietnam War that was responsible for setting in motion many of the groups' activities that would follow.

Despite his campaign pledges to end the war, Nixon continued it for four more years. His rationale was that the United States had to achieve "peace with honor" if its foreign policies were to be credible to the rest of the world. The trouble was that Nixon's "peace with honor" would have meant the virtual capitulation of the Vietcong and the North Vietnamese forces—and, after more than a decade of civil war, this was something that could not be expected.

Nixon then extended the war into Cambodia. Because the eastern border of Cambodia had been used to infiltrate supplies into Vietnam, Nixon unleashed 3,630 massive B-52 sorties against this neutral country. He did so in secret, through a double set of books kept on the progress of the war. On the set of books made available to Congress, the Cambodian raids were listed as raids against Vietnam; only the military and the administration kept track, through a second set of books, of the targets in Cambodia that were really being hit.

Then on May 9, 1969, *The New York Times* broke a front-page story by William Beecher that began: "American B-52 bombers in recent weeks have raided several Vietcong and North Vietnamese supply dumps in Cambodia . . ."

There had been a leak! The Nixon administration panicked. The villain who had "leaked" to Beecher had to be found. The FBI was ordered to wiretap every suspected culprit in sight.

Taps were placed on the telephones of thirteen government officials, including five of Henry Kissinger's closest aides on the National Security Council, and four Washington newsmen. In addition to these FBI taps, on Ehrlichman's order Caulfield hired a Washington private detective to tap the phone of Joseph Kraft, a nationally syndicated columnist and one of the most respected newsmen in Washington. Nixon evidently was suspicious of Kraft because he had tried to get in touch with Kissinger once and had found him having dinner at Kraft's home. The tap turned up nothing and was discontinued after one week. Putting it in in the first place was, however, a flagrantly illegal act carried out on direct orders from the White House by operatives who had no legal status and no court order to justify the tap.

The FBI taps ran for periods ranging from one month to almost two years. They produced no information to show who had leaked the Cambodian raid story to Beecher. These taps had been placed in the name of "national security" and on the contention of John Mitchell that the president could do virtually anything for "national security" reasons. This was an argument that was later struck down by the U.S. Supreme Court, just two days after the Watergate break-in, in fact. The Court ruled 8–0 on June 19, 1972, that no domestic group or individual could be wiretapped without a direct court order.

The crack investigative team of the *London Times* in their book *Watergate* summed up the incident in these words:

> *The issues involved in the wiretapping episode were more than a question of what constituted good manners among friends. For they illustrated how soon the Nixon administration, under the pressure of its Vietnam policy, embarked on a policy of corruption. As early as mid-1969 this corruption operated at three levels. The first was in the decision not to entrust the American people with the true nature of the war policy. The second was in the readiness to deceive the peo-*

ple's elected representatives, even in secret session, about the policy. The third, and ultimately most destructive, was a logical outcome of the first two; they could not trust even themselves . . .

The controversy caused by the secret Cambodian raids was minor compared to that stirred up by Nixon when he went on television on April 30, 1970, to announce that the United States had invaded Cambodia. His justification for the invasion was that the Vietcong had established "sanctuaries" in the Parrot's Beak area northwest of Saigon and that Vietcong headquarters were located in these sanctuaries.

Some arms, rice, and equipment were seized, but the "headquarters," it was found, never existed. This extension of the war into a country that had managed to maintain a precarious peace had two disastrous results, one short-term and one long-lasting. Nixon's action drove Americans opposed to the war almost to the breaking point. And it ensured the eventual destruction of Cambodia—the Cambodian boat people of today are its legacy.

The first reaction had the greater impact on the Nixon administration. More than 400 colleges across the nation closed down or suspended classes in fear of violent protest over the invasion. Student riots and strikes erupted. A furious Nixon called the protestors "bums." It was a word that would haunt him, especially after the Ohio National Guard opened fire on student protestors at Kent State College, killing four and wounding many others, leaving some crippled for life.

American outrage was at a peak. The government seemed out of control of the people (the precise situation the Constitution had been drafted to prevent), and it was dragging the entire nation into the deepening quagmire of a distant war in a country where the United States had no vital national interest.

But Nixon could not accept this view of things. He did not believe that opposition to his war policy was genuine. He felt that American opposition to the war was being inspired and financed by Communist agents from either Russia or China. He ordered the FBI and CIA to dig up the proof. J. Edgar Hoover, then head of the FBI, was a man who could find Communists almost everywhere. His agents infiltrated campuses, youth organizations, protest groups—and came up empty-handed. The CIA likewise could find no proof of foreign involvement in what was really a genuine national protest movement.

Nixon was annoyed and disbelieving. If official agencies couldn't find the proof that he was certain must be there, he would have to establish his own band of undercover agents.

It was in such a mood that he was forced to confront still another event distressing to him. On June 13, 1971, *The New York Times* began publication of the Pentagon Papers, which were a secret official study of the Vietnam War. The study especially exposed the deceitfulness of Lyndon Johnson, who was committed to the war at the very time he was telling the American people otherwise.

Nixon, it would seem, might have turned these disclosures to good political use, citing them as an example of how the previous Democratic administration had hornswoggled the American people. In fact, this seems to have been a tactic that was seriously considered at first. But it was soon abandoned. Overriding all else was the fact that there had been *another leak!*

The source of the leak was soon identified. Daniel Ellsberg, a former government employee, later a consultant with the Rand Corporation, a think-tank employed by the government, had become an opponent of the Vietnam War and had leaked the Pentagon Papers to the *Times*.

The FBI was investigating Ellsberg, but this was not enough for Nixon. He ordered Ehrlichman to set up a White House special investigative unit, separate from the Caulfield-Ulasewicz operation. The unit was established in Room 16, a basement office in the Executive Office Building adjoining the White House. To head it, Ehrlichman chose a protégé of his, Egil Krogh, Jr., a Christian Scientist. Krogh was joined by David Young, a man in his early thirties who was loaned to the project by Henry Kissinger. It was Young who put up a sign on the door of Room 16: "David Young—Plumber."

With the Plumbers (to stop "leaks") established, investigators were needed to do the footwork. Chuck Colson supplied the first one—E. Howard Hunt. A slight, sandy-haired man of medium height, Hunt had written a number of spy novels and was working for the Robert H. Mullen Company, a Washington, D.C. public relations firm with close Republican ties. What appealed to Colson, apparently, was Hunt's burning hatred of the Kennedys. He blamed President Kennedy for the failure of the Bay of Pigs invasion, and he was willing to do almost anything to tar the Kennedys. The result was that Colson asked the Mullen firm to let Hunt "moonlight" for the White House, and so Hunt became a $100-a-day consultant for Colson. When the Plumbers unit was set up, he joined the boys in Room 16.

There he combined forces with G. Gordon Liddy. Liddy had been employed in the Treasury Department's Operation Intercept, designed to try to stop the flow of heroin and marijuana across the Mexican border. He had impressed Egil Krogh, who was coordinating the White House end of Operation Intercept; but Liddy's superiors in Treasury were not so pleased. They found him unpredictable and uncontrollable—and fired him. Krogh promptly brought him to work for the Plumbers.

In such fashion had the stage been set. One step had led to another and then another. Throughout runs a theme of paranoia. Fear of losing the 1972 election had led to the use of the Kalmbach secret fund in the Alabama primary and the hiring of Colson to head a "dirty tricks" brigade. But "dirty tricks" weren't enough. The leaks of the Pentagon Papers and the details of the secret Cambodian air raids intensified the paranoia in a White House that already felt it was surrounded by enemies and victimized by spies in its own ranks. These foes had to be dealt with, and so the FBI was ordered to conduct wiretapping that the U.S. Supreme

Court would later rule illegal. Even the wiretapping wasn't enough. Because neither the FBI nor the CIA could find any trace of the subversives who, the White House felt, *must* be fomenting the Vietnam War protests, yet another and fateful step was taken: the Plumbers were established to serve the White House outside the law and do things that the FBI and CIA couldn't legally do. And when the White House finally united the volatile and erratic Liddy with the imaginative and vengeful Hunt, they set in motion a combination guaranteed to spell disaster.

CHAPTER

THE
BREWING STORM

John Dean, flying back from halfway around the world, had no idea of the cyclone of apprehension that was sweeping through administration circles. Fagged out from jet lag, he was at the moment far removed from the turmoil caused by the cast of characters brought together by the Nixon White House and CREEP. But back in Washington, down at Key Biscayne, and out in California, telephones were almost jumping off their hooks.

John Ehrlichman was hit with the first rumblings of the brewing storm. On Saturday afternoon, June 17, the day of the Watergate burglary, he got a telephone call from Secret Service Agent Pat Boggs. Boggs told him that police had found a notebook on one of the burglars listing the name of a White House employee, E. Howard Hunt.

Ehrlichman hadn't had time to digest this news when his phone rang again. Jack Caulfield, the first of the White House's undercover men, was calling with the same message. "My God," Caulfield later recalled Ehrlichman saying, "you know, I can't believe it."

Caulfield's call to Ehrlichman triggered a telephonic circus. Ehrlichman phoned Ron Ziegler in Key Biscayne to pass the word to Haldeman and the president. Long-distance calls began to zip one after the other across the nation—Haldeman calling Magruder and Mitchell in California; Ehrlichman telephoning Chuck Colson and Haldeman; the president calling Colson from Key Biscayne on three separate occasions.

In the midst of this mass confusion, a bewildered John Dean arrived home from the airport. His first impulse was to suspect that the Watergate fiasco had been engineered by Colson. It was not an irrational thought; Dean knew that Colson had once wanted to firebomb the Brookings Institution, a prestigious Washington think-tank.

That bit of aborted madness had stemmed from the Pentagon Papers furor. Morton Halperin, who had been an assistant to Henry Kissinger and one of those whose phones had been tapped, had left the National Security Council and become a consultant at Brookings. The White House suspected that he had ties to Daniel Ellsberg and that there might be further leaks as damaging to Nixon as the Pentagon Papers had been to Lyndon Johnson.

Colson had sent Jack Caulfield to study the possibility of breaking into the Brookings Institution to get Halperin's papers. When Caulfield reported that such a burglary seemed impossible, Colson wanted him to firebomb the place and try to get the records in the resulting confusion. Caulfield had been so horrified by the idea that he had appealed to Dean, who had gotten Ehrlichman to scotch the plan.

Dean was also aware (because Caulfield had told him with considerable relish) that in one of the first adventures of the Plumbers, Hunt and Liddy had burglarized the Los Angeles office of Dr. Lewis Fielding, Ellsberg's psychiatrist. The intention had been to dig up some dirt about Ellsberg that could be used to discredit him. The Hunt-Liddy team, using some of the same Cubans later caught in the Watergate complex, had succeeded in breaking into the psychiatrist's office; they had pulled out files and messed up the place—but had found nothing that would help in the contemplated character assassination of Ellsberg.

Knowledge of such past illegal adventures had still not prepared Dean for the blizzard of telephone calls that hit him almost the moment he walked into his White House office on Monday morning, June 19. Caulfield phoned in a panic because he had recommended McCord for his job as security director of CREEP. Jeb Magruder was next. It was all Liddy's fault, he said; it was "a PR problem" that could be handled—maybe. Magruder ran on and on like a man so shaken he couldn't stop talking, and Dean was only able to get him off the phone by telling him that John Ehrlichman was calling.

Ehrlichman said he had talked to Colson, who vowed that he had had nothing to do with the Watergate break-in. What about E. Howard Hunt? Why, Colson hardly knew the man. Ehrlichman didn't trust Colson's avowed innocence and wanted Dean to see if he could find out more from Colson. It would be a good idea for Dean to see and talk to Liddy, too.

Dean phoned Colson, who was still positioning himself as far away from E. Howard Hunt as possible. Then Dean called Attorney General Kleindienst, who was still smarting from his Saturday encounter with Liddy. He told Dean coolly, "The investigation is proceeding as it should."

Getting nowhere with Kleindienst, Dean contacted Liddy. The two men met and took a walk in the streets. Liddy confessed it was all his fault. He never should have taken McCord on the Watergate job; the tie-in with the president's campaign was too close. As they prepared to part, Liddy startled Dean by saying, "This is my fault. I'm prepared to accept responsibility for it. And if somebody wants to shoot me on a streetcorner I'm prepared to have that done. You just let me know when and where, and I'll be there."

Shocked almost speechless, Dean murmured some

parting words and headed back to his office. He had barely seated himself and started to eat a cup of soup when he looked up and saw Gordon Strachan standing in his doorway. Strachan was Haldeman's deputy in the White House. He was young, blond, and fair-skinned.

Strachan told Dean that, acting on instructions from Haldeman, he had "cleaned out" all of Haldeman's files over the weekend. The files had included the wiretap logs he had received and a set of political instructions from Haldeman to Liddy to concentrate his activities on Senator McGovern, the Democratic nominee. Strachan had taken out "everything sensitive and shredded it."

Dean had hardly gotten Strachan out of his office when his phone rang again. Hugh Sloan, the young treasurer of CREEP, was on the line. He was a very worried young man. He just wanted Dean to know that he had given Liddy bundles of cash. He hadn't known at the time what the money was for, but now he had read about those $100 bills that had been found in the Watergate burglary. Could there be fingerprints on those bills? Would he be responsible for a Campaign Act violation? Dean tried to reassure him.

Then Dean went to see Ehrlichman. When he told Ehrlichman about his conversations, he mentioned Liddy's offer to be shot on the street. Ehrlichman commented, "That's interesting." Aside from this, he was poker-faced throughout most of the interview. Dean mentioned that Colson wanted to meet with both of them, and Ehrlichman suggested they see him at 4:30 that afternoon. At this meeting, Colson tried to put as much distance as possible between himself and Hunt. He said he had no idea where Hunt was. Ehrlichman, Dean later said, suggested that it might be a good idea to telephone Liddy and tell him to get Hunt out of the country.

Dean followed these instructions, but after he phoned Liddy his legal mind began to have second thoughts. He suggested to Ehrlichman that it might make things worse if Hunt were on the lam. Ehrlichman agreed, and Dean countermanded the order he had just given to Liddy.

In the meantime Bob Woodward of the *Washington Post* had taken up Hunt's trail. He dialed the White House and asked for Mr. Hunt. The switchboard operator apparently found nothing unusual in the request; she just rang a number. There was no answer. Woodward was about to hang up when the operator said helpfully, "There's one other place he might be. In Mr. Colson's office."

She rang Colson's number and Colson's secretary told Woodward, "Mr. Hunt is not here now." Then she suggested that Woodward might try the Robert H. Mullen advertising agency. Woodward dialed the number and a voice answered, "Howard Hunt here." Woodward identified himself, then asked Hunt why his name and White House connection were in the address books of two men arrested at the Watergate complex.

"Good God!" Hunt exclaimed involuntarily. Then he regained his composure and said he would make no comment because the case was in the courts. He slammed down the phone.

Still hot on the trail, Woodward telephoned Ken W. Clawson, a former *Post* reporter who had left to become deputy director of communications at the White House. He told Clawson what he knew, and Clawson said he would check.

Events had reached this stage by the time Colson, Dean, and Ehrlichman met in Ehrlichman's office at 4:30 that day. Dean told Colson he had tried to check employment records, and it seemed that Hunt was still on Colson's payroll. Colson shrilly denied it and suggested that Clawson be brought into the meeting because he was being asked questions by Woodward about Hunt.

While they were waiting for Clawson, Colson said, almost apologetically, that there was one more point he should perhaps bring up. And that was that Hunt had "a safe in the White House up in his office." Ehrlichman,

Dean wrote later, appeared completely astonished by this news.

When Clawson arrived, the conferees mapped out a reply that should be given to the *Post*. They decided to just say that Hunt had worked as a consultant on the declassification of the Pentagon Papers and on a narcotics intelligence problem. But he had last been paid as a consultant on March 29 and had had no connection with the White House recently.

Clawson promptly parroted the party line to Woodward, but he was so eager to add his own assurances—and this without any prompting—that he only made Woodward more suspicious.

Back in Ehrlichman's office, they were dealing with the knotty problem posed by E. Howard Hunt's White House safe. Ehrlichman decided they should get men in from the General Services Administration (GSA) to open the safe—and that Dean should then take charge of the contents.

CHAPTER

THE GOING
GETS ROUGHER

If Monday had been a day when it seemed as if the White House walls were about to cave in, Tuesday was even worse. That morning the *Washington Post* carried Ron Ziegler's bland statement from Key Biscayne: "I am not going to comment from the White House on a third-rate burglary attempt. It is as simple as that." It was not, of course, "as simple as that," for the *Washington Post* in the same edition splashed Woodward's story on E. Howard Hunt on page one under a headline that read: "White House Consultant Linked to Burglary Suspects."

Things got worse even before the morning was half over. The Democratic National Committee filed a $1 million civil lawsuit against CREEP and the Republican National Committee. Lawrence O'Brien, the principal target of the Watergate bugging, charged that the evidence was developing "a clear line to the White House."

"I believe," he said, "we are about to witness the ultimate test of this administration that so piously committed itself to a new era of law and order just four years ago."

O'Brien ridiculed Mitchell's attempt to put a safe distance between the White House and James McCord. "We know that as of the moment of his arrest at gunpoint just ten feet from where I now stand," O'Brien said, "Mr. McCord was in the pay of the Committee to Re-Elect the President."

Edward Bennett Williams, one of the most formidable trial lawyers in the nation and the treasurer of the Democratic National Committee, was going to handle the suit. Mitchell responded by calling the suit "a publicity stunt," but every insider in the Nixon administration knew that it could not be so lightly dismissed.

John Dean knew better than most because, even as O'Brien was speaking, he was wrestling with the contents of Hunt's opened safe. GSA employees had wheeled dollies containing cartons full of the safe's contents into Dean's office.

Before Dean could sort the stuff, however, he was summoned to Ehrlichman's office. Haldeman had returned from Florida with the president. Mitchell was present, and Kleindienst soon joined them. Dean later wrote that he had expected some serious discussion of their problems, but it soon became obvious that no one wanted to talk about what *he* knew. Ehrlichman made the only decision, that all questions about Watergate should be referred to Mitchell.

After the meeting, Dean went back to the attorney general's office with Kleindienst. Both were worried about where Watergate might lead, but Kleindienst refused to stop an investigation once started. There were, however, some indications that the Justice Department might be willing to help put a lid on where the investigation went.

Kleindienst brought in Henry E. Petersen, head of the criminal division, a man who had risen through the ranks by sheer merit. Petersen told Dean that Earl Silbert, an assistant U.S. attorney, was in charge of the case. He added that Silbert had been told he was just investigating a break-in; he wasn't to look for anything else.

Reassured, Dean returned to his office, where he was soon confronted with a new problem. Gordon Strachan appeared again, this time accompanied by Dick Howard, a Colson aide. Colson, Howard said, had been given campaign funds to sponsor some questionable political advertising, and a smear campaign Colson had masterminded had resulted in the 1970 defeat of Senator Joseph Tydings, a liberal Maryland Democrat. Colson had also used some of the money for pro-war ads headlined "Tell It to Hanoi," purportedly coming from supporters of Nixon's war policy but not carrying any identification of the sponsors. Strachan and Howard had become concerned that such misuse of campaign funds might have violated election laws. They had a bulging envelope with them. In the envelope was $15,200 left over from the Colson fund. Would Dean keep it for them? Dean took the envelope, marked the amount on it, and put it in his safe. It was obvious to him by this time that everyone was running scared and dumping on someone else if they could. Dean's office, it seemed, was becoming everybody's favorite dumping ground.

After Strachan and Howard left, Dean turned to Hunt's treasure trove. Fred Fielding, his assistant, suggested that they don surgical gloves so that they would leave no fingerprints. One box was filled with ordinary odds-and-ends—stationery, pencils, paper clips. But a metal container that looked like a fishing box contained a revolver. Another carton contained a stack of documents nearly a foot high.

These were State Department cables dealing with the early stages of the Vietnam War. Included in the lot was a phony State Department cable falsely indicating that President Kennedy had ordered the assassination of South Vietnam's dictatorial president, Ngo Dinh Diem. This had been a favorite project for Colson and Hunt. Hunt had taken a series of legitimate State Department cables and pieced parts of them together to create a forgery. With Hunt's masterpiece were memos that had passed between Hunt and Colson about how to plant the false story with William Lambert of *Life* magazine. (This attempt had, indeed, been made.

But when Colson refused to give Lambert a copy of the fraudulent cable, Lambert had refused to touch the story.)

Hunt's hoard also included a black briefcase filled with bugging equipment and several folders of potentially explosive political material. One folder contained a psychological profile of Daniel Ellsberg. Dean and Fielding locked the gun and bugging equipment in Dean's closet and put the folders of "sensitive" political material in Dean's safe.

The day's bombshells still did not stop exploding. Late in the afternoon Jeb Magruder visited Dean's office and told him that John Mitchell had approved some of Liddy's wild schemes at a meeting in Florida. Dean later testified about his knowledge of Liddy's original $1 million proposal for underground political warfare; but he had not known until Magruder told him that Mitchell had approved a scaled-down version of that proposal that led directly to the Watergate break-in.

With this information, it became clear to Dean that virtually everyone in the highest ranks of the administration, everyone close to the president, was involved. Liddy led to Mitchell, and Mitchell led to the president. Gordon Strachan and his shredding machine led to Haldeman, and Haldeman led to the president. Colson led to Ehrlichman, and Ehrlichman led to the president. Everybody in the whole administration, it seemed, was involved.

At another meeting in Mitchell's apartment that night, the mood was glum. No one wanted to talk about the things they all knew. The discussion centered on public relations gimmicks by which "the problem" might be "handled."

Afterward, Robert Mardian took Dean to his apartment. The former assistant attorney general was badly shaken. He, like Dean, had talked to Gordon Liddy. Liddy had not yet been connected to the scandal, and he had seemed confident he would not be. Mardian was not so sure.

Liddy had told Mardian that the members of his team were all "soldiers;" they would not talk. But certain "commitments" would have to be honored. Their legal bills would have to be paid, their families helped financially.

The plain implication was that there would have to be a payoff for silence.

Mardian was appalled. So was Dean. As lawyers, both knew that the payment of "hush-money," as it was called, would lay everyone involved open to the criminal charge of obstruction of justice. Neither shared Liddy's confidence that his role in the Watergate break-in would not be exposed. There was one trail of hard evidence that led directly to CREEP and to Liddy—the trail left behind by those fresh $100 bills, all consecutively numbered.

CHAPTER
10
THOSE
TELLTALE CHECKS

On this same Tuesday, June 20, while Mardian and Dean were worrying about the connections that might be established through those $100 bills, the FBI was discovering the source of those bills. The FBI's Miami field office, running down all leads on the Cuban Watergate burglars, came across the bank account of their leader, Bernard Barker.

For an exiled Cuban businessman, Barker had handled suspiciously large sums of money. FBI agents found that, on April 20, $114,000 had been deposited in his bank account. The bank supplied copies of the original checks. Four of them had been signed by a Manuel Ogarrio Daguerre on a Mexican bank, the fifth by a man named Kenneth Dahlberg. The information was sent to Washington headquarters where, since J. Edgar Hoover had recently died, Nixon loyalist L. Patrick Gray was acting director of the FBI.

Gray had this information about the mysterious Barker bank account on June 21 when Dean came to see him. Dean told the FBI chief that he had been instructed to keep abreast of the investigation for the White House, and Gray told him about the leads that had been uncovered in Miami.

Though Gray himself didn't know what to make of the information, the news was highly disturbing to Dean. He knew that the trail of the checks, if followed carefully, would lead directly to the door of CREEP.

Some explanation is necessary here. A new federal campaign financing law had gone into effect April 7. It provided that the names of large donors to a presidential campaign must be disclosed. Prior to the April 7 date, however, there was no such provision. Nixon fund raisers conducted a whirlwind campaign to raise millions of dollars before the April 7 disclosure date. When campaign contributions came in after that date, they were "laundered" by being routed through the Mexican connection, then via Barker into the hands of CREEP. This kept contributors who wanted to remain anonymous happy.

The Nixon campaign drive ended up raising some $60 million, about $22 million of it illegally. But it was this Mexican-Barker bank connection that was the most explosive; for it was this money, transferred by CREEP to Liddy, that had furnished the $100 bills found on the Watergate burglars.

Gray's information that the FBI was sniffing on this dangerous trail was disconcerting news to the White House. But there was, perhaps, one salvation. Gray was uncertain what the Mexican connection meant. Since the Watergate burglars had had close ties with the CIA, Gray telephoned CIA Director Richard Helms to determine whether the CIA had been involved in the Watergate break-in. Helms told him that it had not.

Dean thought, however, that the CIA red herring could be potentially valuable to the White House cover-up effort. And so, on the evening of June 22, Dean returned to see Gray and play upon his suspicions of a possible CIA connection. Gray later recalled Dean's hinting that an investigation of the Mexican checks might uncover a sensitive CIA operation.

Nixon's tapes subsequently revealed how eagerly he and Haldeman had discussed this ploy as a means of stopping the FBI. The conversation took place on the morning of June 23. Haldeman told the president that both Dean and Mitchell recommended using the CIA to put a lid on the FBI probe. Then, from the tape:

HALDEMAN: And you seem to think the thing to do is to get them [the FBI] to stop?
PRESIDENT: Right. Fine.
HALDEMAN: They say the only way to do that is from White House instructions. And it's got to be Helms and to ah . . . Walters. And the proposal should be that Ehrlichman and I call them in, and say, ah—
PRESIDENT: All right, fine . . . Well, we protected Helms from a helluva lot of things . . . Play it tough. That's the way they play it and that's the way we're going to play it.

They then discussed the need to protect John Mitchell. The whole exchange lasted probably less than five minutes, but in this short time Richard Nixon committed a criminal act. Here was a person who had taken an oath to "preserve, protect, and defend the Constitution of the United States" and to see that its laws were faithfully enforced. Instead, he was now plotting with his aides to prevent the enforcement of the law. One of the oldest definitions of crime in both English and American law is "misprison of felony." The term comes from an old French word meaning "to make a mistake," and it applies to officials in this manner, that an official is guilty if he or she should be able to recognize a crime but either fails to do so or fails to bring it to court.

There could be no question here that Nixon recognized what was involved and that, not only was he failing to bring it to court, he was actively engaged in trying to block the investigation. As a lawyer, Nixon should have been aware that he was laying himself open to one of the oldest criminal charges in American jurisprudence, but he ignored the danger. It was just the first of many times that he would do so. Why would he take such a risk? The answer seems to lie in Nixon's concept of the powers of the presidency. He seems to have considered the presidency a law unto itself, to believe that the president had the power to do anything he wished (as in ordering the illegal wiretapping) without ever being brought to justice for his misdeeds.

In this atmosphere, Nixon and his aides discussed the best way to use the CIA to block the FBI probe. They decided that their agent should be Deputy Director Lieutenant General Vernon Walters, a Nixon loyalist who had been installed in the CIA to keep an eye on Helms. Walters was eager to please, and, on this same afternoon of June 23, he went to see Gray. He urged the FBI to suspend its investigation until the CIA could find out whether vital national security issues were involved.

The ploy worked for only a few days. Helms, Walters, and Gray all struggled with what was being asked of them. Helms, it seems, was determined from the outset not to let the CIA become involved, and so the administration's plan to use Walters as its intermediary was foiled. Walters wrote and kept memoranda. They tell of the CIA's flat refusal to be drawn into the illegal cover-up. Walters finally told Dean there was no CIA-Mexican connection and that "the Agency was not in any way involved."

When Dean reported this to Ehrlichman, Ehrlichman told him to try harder. Dean recalled Ehrlichman's saying something like, "General Walters seems to have forgotten how he got where he is today."

Acting Director Gray was having his own problems. The stalled investigation worried his conscientious agents. They kept pressing him to let them interview the mysterious Ogarrio. On June 27 Gray telephoned Helms and asked him directly if the FBI should hold off because of the CIA's interest in Ogarrio. Helms said the CIA had no interest. Seven minutes later, Gray later testified, Dean phoned him and again asked the FBI to stay away from Ogarrio and Dahlberg because of "CIA interest in these men."

If Gray's head was whirling from these contradictory signals, one could hardly blame him. In the meantime Dean, carrying out Ehrlichman's order to try harder, summoned Walters to the White House. Wasn't there some way the CIA could express at least a slight interest in these men? Walters told him there was not.

Then Dean, according to the memoranda Walters made at the time, advanced an even more preposterous suggestion. He wanted to know whether the CIA could make funds available from its unchecked budget to pay hush-money to the Watergate defendants. Walters was appalled. He said he had no authority to do any such thing. "I said I realized that he [Dean] had a very tough problem, but if there were Agency involvement, it could only be at presidential directive, and the political risks that were concomitant appeared to be unacceptable."

All of this was, of course, unknown to the public at the time. It remained so until late July, when those energetic *Washington Post* reporters, Woodward and Bernstein, uncovered the check-laundering scandal.

District Attorney Richard Gerstein, a Democrat running for reelection in Miami, had begun his own independent investigation as soon as he noticed the Cuban-Miami connection with Watergate. His chief investigator Martin Dardis, a former New York State trooper, tracked down the trail of the money; and reporter Bernstein, going to Miami, obtained a copy of his records. Bernstein was especially intrigued by the $25,000 Kenneth Dahlberg check. Who was Dahlberg?

Woodward found out. Dahlberg was a Minneapolis businessman and a partner of Dwayne Andreas, a Minnesota grain tycoon and former supporter of Democrat Hubert Humphrey. Andreas and Dahlberg wanted a charter for a new bank, and so they had made a $25,000 contribution to the Nixon campaign. (They got the bank.)

The check had been delivered after the April 7 deadline and was whitewashed by being funneled through Barker's bank account. Dahlberg told Woodward that he had given the check to either Hugh Sloan or Maurice Stans in the finance office of CREEP. The *Post* broke the story on page one.

The following day Philip S. Hughes, director of the new Federal Elections Division of the General Accounting Office (GAO), the federal auditing agency for Congress, began an investigation. He told Woodward that the *Post's* Dahlberg story was the first indication that "the bugging incident was related to the campaign finance law. . . . There's nothing in Maury's [Stans'] reports showing anything like that Dahlberg check."

Almost a month later, on August 26, the GAO report was released. It listed eleven "apparent and possible violations" of the new election law. The report said that Maurice Stans had maintained a "slush fund" of at least $350,000 in his office in CREEP—a fund that had at one time contained the Dahlberg check and the four Mexican checks—and that the money found on the Watergate burglars had come from this fund. It asked the Justice Department to investigate.

The GAO report was issued just three days after Nixon had been renominated. On the surface the president appeared to have smooth sailing all the way to reelection, but the GAO report was just one indication of troubles brewing. There were others.

E. Howard Hunt, who had hidden out for ten days with a friend in California, had 150 FBI agents searching for him and had finally come in and given himself up. Gordon Liddy had also been exposed. FBI agents had found the name "George" with a telephone number beside it in the Cuban Eugenio Martinez's address book. When they checked out the number, they came up with the name of George Gordon Liddy.

The FBI had tried to question Liddy, but he refused to be interviewed. John Mitchell then fired him as counsel for CREEP. All of this happened at the end of June, but Liddy's dismissal remained secret for almost a month.

Then, on July 22, the Long Island newspaper *Newsday* broke the story of Liddy's ouster and his possible connection with the Watergate burglary.

By that time, John Mitchell himself was long gone from CREEP.

CHAPTER
11
MARTHA TALKS

Martha Mitchell, wife of John Mitchell, was one of the most volatile and outspoken women ever to hit Washington. Her volubility was legendary and made many consider her whacky.

Martha was with her husband on the Hollywood campaign trip when the Watergate scandal broke. John departed hurriedly for Washington on Monday morning after persuading her to stay on in California for a few days. Before he left he read the Monday morning papers, then threw them away.

Martha sent her security guard, Steve King, to get her another set of newspapers. Reading them, she learned for the first time about Watergate and her husband's official statement about Jim McCord.

According to a deposition Martha later gave her lawyer, she was stunned and didn't know what to believe. "My first thought," she said, "was that McCord had been a double agent." Then she read her husband's statement again and began to worry. She knew that John Mitchell had been less than honest in trying to convey the impression that McCord might have been working for some client other than CREEP when he entered the Watergate.

In a daze, she said, she telephoned her husband asking for an explanation. She could not recall afterward precisely what he said, but the conversation left her frightened and worried. She could see a pit yawning for John Mitchell whom, it seems, in spite of her "whackiness," she really loved.

Martha remained silent until Thursday. By this time, apparently, she had decided in her own mind that she would have to get John Mitchell out of politics before he was ruined. She had developed a habit of making late-night phone calls to Helen Thomas, United Press International's White House correspondent, and she decided that the best way to get John Mitchell out of politics was to create a public outcry.

Politics was "a dirty business," she told Thomas, and if John didn't get out, "I will leave him." At this point, Thomas wrote, the conversation ended suddenly "when it appeared that somebody had taken the telephone from her hand."

Martha Mitchell's version, as she later gave it, was much more graphic. Steve King, she said, rushed into her room and yanked the phone away from her. Then he ripped the phone out of the wall and similarly ripped out all the other phones in the motel villa where they were staying.

For three days, she later claimed, King kept her a virtual prisoner. When she protested too shrilly, she said, he flung her down on the bed and a doctor injected a sedative into her, knocking her out.

Back in Washington, when Thomas's story broke, John Mitchell attempted to laugh it off. He was "amused," he said, that his wife had resumed her telephone talks. As for politics—well, he intended to get out of politics after the campaign anyway. Others in the administration were not laughing. They strove hard to portray Martha as an alcoholic who would say almost anything. Most of Washington, knowing Martha as it did, tended to go along with John and laugh the matter off as just another example of her eccentricity.

The laughter faded a bit, however, when Martha finally got free and made it to a phone to call Helen Thomas again. She had been kept a prisoner all week, she said, because her husband and his associates were "afraid of my honesty." (Incidentally, this *was* the week that her husband was using their Watergate apartment for those secret conferences on how to "PR" and contain the Watergate affair.) Martha gave Helen Thomas a graphic description of her rough treatment and imprisonment and announced, "I won't stand for this dirty business."

Mitchell reacted by flying to California and bringing Martha back. And on July 1, 1972, just fourteen days after Watergate, he resigned as director of **CREEP**. "I found that I can no longer [carry out the job] and still meet the one obligation that must come first: the happiness and welfare of my wife and daughter," his statement said. He added that politics imposes a heavy strain on the families of politicians.

This devoted-husband pose pulled the wool over the public's eyes at the time, and the whole Martha-John Mitchell affair was dismissed as just one of those matrimonial spats. But the evidence says that much more was involved.

Mitchell's resignation followed closely on the FBI's discovery of the identity and importance of G. Gordon Liddy. The Liddy trail, it was clear, would lead almost inevitably to Mitchell, the man who had approved his espionage schemes. The resignation also came, as the Watergate investigation later showed, immediately after a conference at the White House. According to Fred LaRue, Mitchell's closest aide at **CREEP**, there was no indication that Mitchell had any intention of resigning when he left for the White House on June 30. Among the White House tapes is one covering this June 30 conference. Present were Nixon, Mitchell, and Haldeman.

Haldeman tells Mitchell:
"The longer you wait, the more risk each hour brings. You run the risk of more stuff, valid or invalid, surfacing on the Watergate-caper type of thing. . . . As of now there is no problem there. As, as of any moment in the future there is at least a potential problem."
Nixon chimes in:
"Well, I'd cut the loss fast. I'd cut it fast. If we're going to do it I'd cut it fast. That's my view, generally speaking . . . I think the story is you're positive rather than negative. . . . A hell of a lot of people will like that answer. They would. And it'd make anybody else who asked any other question look like a selfish [expletive], which I thoroughly intend them to look like."

And so John Mitchell, former law partner and closest friend of the president during the revival of Nixon's political fortunes, was told to walk the plank. Loyally, he did. And the American people swallowed the fantasy that he did it all for Martha.

But Martha herself was not deceived. It was not long before John Mitchell walked out on her and their marriage broke up. Still, Martha did not stop talking. She always referred to Nixon as *"Mr. President,"* with real scorn in her voice. She threatened many times that "Mr. President" would be sorry if she ever told all she knew. But she never produced any startling information.

CHAPTER
12
THE "DEAN REPORT"

From the very moment of the Watergate arrests, the Nixon administration had just one plan: cover-up. What even Mitchell would later call "the White House horrors" had to be concealed from the American public until after the election. As Jeb Stuart Magruder later testified, no thought was ever given to any other line of action. The cover-up process was instinctive; and once it began, there was no end to it.

Maintenance of the cover-up required three basic lines of action. First, the investigation had to be stopped at the level of Hunt and Liddy; and this meant that the contents of Hunt's safe could never come to light and the trail of $100 bills could go no higher than Jeb Magruder's level at CREEP. Second, potential witnesses had to be close-mouthed; they had to be coached not to volunteer informa-tion—and even how to commit perjury if necessary. Third, and most immediately important, hush-money had to be raised for the Watergate Seven to make certain that none of them talked.

The key manipulator of all three phases of the conspiracy was John Dean, counsel to the president.

The hush-money problem became acute when Hunt, only days after the break-in, passed a message to Dean with the blunt warning, "The writer has a manuscript to sell." On June 28 a high-level conference was held in Mitchell's office in CREEP. Present were Mitchell, Dean, Fred LaRue, and Mardian. All agreed, according to Dean, that it was imperative to raise "support money in exchange for the silence of the men in jail."

As the meeting ended Mitchell said to Dean, in a voice so low that none of the others could hear, that "the White House, and in particular John Ehrlichman, would be very interested to accommodate the needs of these men." Mitchell was shoving the nasty job off on Ehrlichman, who had been responsible for the Plumbers' operations.

Dean talked to Ehrlichman and Haldeman later the same day, and it was decided to call in Herbert Kalmbach, the president's personal counsel and custodian of the 1968 $2 million fund. Kalmbach flew in from Los Angeles, and he and Dean plotted their course on a bench in Lafayette Park. Dean said they would have to raise between $50,000 and $100,000.

Kalmbach accepted the task with reluctance. First, he telephoned Maury Stans, the campaign treasurer. Could Stans help? It just so happened that he could. He had $75,000 just lying around, and within hours he had delivered to Kalmbach a bundle of $100 bills. The source of this money has remained a mystery.

What followed was high farce. The president's White House counsel and the president's personal counsel met on park benches like Mafia conspirators to decide how to deliver the money. They settled on the use of cryptic aliases. When they talked on the phone, "the Brush" would mean Haldeman because of his close-cropped hair. "The Pipe" was John Mitchell. "Brows" meant Ehrlichman, with his distinctive forehead furrows. "Mr. Rivers" would refer to

Tony Ulasewicz, Jack Caulfield's partner and the man chosen to deliver the money. "The Writer's Wife" meant Mrs. E. Howard Hunt, and "The Script" referred to the money.

Ulasewicz had the most difficult task of all. He had to find ways of delivering the hush-money so that he could not be seen and later identified. One of his trickiest problems after Kalmbach had given him Stans's $75,000 was making contact with Hunt's lawyer, William O. Bittman. Bittman was a former federal prosecutor and a member of one of Washington's most distinguished law firms.

When "Mr. Rivers" phoned Bittman to find out how much "Script" he wanted, the lawyer told him huffily that he didn't do business that way. Ulasewicz couldn't get anywhere with him and had to lug his $75,000 in a brown paper bag back home to New York.

There followed a flurry of phone calls and several days' delay. "Mr. Rivers" carried his bundle back and forth, desperate, as he later said, "to get rid of all those cookies." He had to make so many long-distance phone calls from pay booths that he bought a motorman's coin box in which to carry his change; and once, while waiting in line to take a shuttle flight back to New York, he noticed that the baggage of some of the passengers ahead of him was being searched. Ulasewicz, clutching his brown paper bag in his arms, ducked out of the line and took the train.

Finally, he got word from Kalmbach that matters had been explained to Bittman. Ulasewicz telephoned the attorney again, and Bittman said his fee would be $25,000. Informed of this, Kalmbach said, in effect, "All right, pay him in any manner you see fit."

Ulasewicz jaunted back to Washington. He counted out $25,000 from his bag of "cookies," placed the bills in a brown paper envelope, and then phoned Bittman from a telephone in the lobby of the lawyer's building. He told Bittman to come right down to the lobby and pick up the brown envelope he would find lying on a shelf by the pay phone. Just to make certain the right man got the envelope, Ulasewicz asked Bittman what color suit he was wearing. "Brown," Bittman said. A few minutes later Ulasewicz, watching from a distance, saw a man in a brown suit enter the lobby, grab the envelope, and hustle back upstairs.

In his role as "Mr. Rivers" Ulasewicz had an easier time with "The Writer's Wife." He had observed that the end telephone booth in the American Airlines terminal of Washington National Airport was seldom used. So he would rent a locker, put the hush-money inside, then tape the key directly under the coin box of the telephone in this little-used booth. He would call Mrs. Hunt to come to the airport at a specific time and watch while she went to the phone booth, retrieved the key, and picked up the money.

The first delivery went off smoothly, but Mrs. Hunt was not happy. She had collected a piddling $40,000; she needed $130,000, she said. She was making the payoffs to all the other defendants, and they had legal fees to meet, wives and families to support—$40,000 wouldn't begin to be enough.

Kalmbach and Ulasewicz became alarmed as the demands mounted. Kalmbach raised more money. He delivered another $40,000 to Ulasewicz in New York's Regency Hotel; $28,000 in the Hilton Hotel in Washington; and a final $75,000 at the Airporter Inn in Los Angeles—a grand total of $219,000.

Still, it wasn't enough to meet Mrs. Hunt's ever-increasing demands. Ulasewicz and Kalmbach estimated that she wanted between $400,000 and $450,000. At this point they both became alarmed and quit. Let someone else take over the hush-money deal.

They had, however, temporarily tamped down one of the major problems. An equally worrisome one in this cover-up summer of 1972 was what to do with the documents and electronic equipment found in Hunt's White House safe.

Ehrlichman advised Dean to shred the sensitive political material—the phony State Department cable libeling President Kennedy in the Diem assassination, the material about the break-in of Ellsberg's psychiatrist's office, and research material on Ted Kennedy's accident at Chappaquiddick in which Mary Jo Kopechne had drowned. As for the wiretapping data, Ehrlichman advised Dean to "deep six" it. Dean asked what he meant. As Dean later recounted the story (Ehrlichman insisted he couldn't recall any of it), Ehrlichman leaned back in his chair and said: "You drive across the river on your way home every night, don't you?"

"Yes," Dean replied.

"Well, when you cross over the bridge on your way home, just toss the briefcase into the river."

Dean reminded Ehrlichman that he, too, drove across the bridge. Wouldn't he like to do the job? "No thanks," Ehrlichman said.

This deliberate destruction of evidence worried young Mr. Dean. He was already involved in illegal capers but had not yet done anything as serious as this. He put Hunt's briefcase in the back of his car and for several days drove back and forth across the Potomac, unable to bring himself to "deep six" the evidence.

He sought another solution—and found one. He was constantly in touch with FBI Acting Director Gray. He had put pressure on Gray to let him see FBI records of interviews that agents were conducting during the investigation. Gray had asked if this order had come from the president, and Dean had indicated that it had. And Gray, the ultimate loyalist, believing as others in the inner circle did that the skies would fall if Nixon were not reelected, had let Dean have the secret FBI reports.

So partisan was Gray that the investigation the FBI conducted hardly deserved the name. Instead of questioning witnesses in their homes or calling them in for questioning, FBI agents interviewed them in the offices of CREEP, usually with Dean sitting in to monitor the interview.

Thus, Dean was present on June 22 when the FBI questioned Chuck Colson. Agents asked if Hunt had occupied an office in the White House. Colson had to admit that he had. The agents naturally wanted to see the office. Dean stalled them by pretending surprise at this information and saying that he would have to check which office it was and let them know.

The agents were persistent. They kept asking to see the office and its contents. Something had to be done. Dean went to Ehrlichman. He told Ehrlichman that too many people knew about Hunt's safe—the GSA men who had opened it, Secret Service men, his own assistant, his secretary, and God-only-knew who else. With knowledge so general, they couldn't get away with destroying evidence.

The answer, Dean suggested, was a two-pronged ploy. Give the FBI agents the electronic equipment and the files that didn't matter. Then turn the rest—the politically "sensitive" material—over to Gray. That way they could say that everything had been given to the FBI.

On June 28, Pat Gray was called to Ehrlichman's office. Dean was there with two folders containing the details of "the White House horrors." Dean and Ehrlichman told Gray that the material had come from Hunt's files, but that it had nothing to do with Watergate. The documents, however, could be "political dynamite" in an election year. Gray later recalled Dean's telling him "they should never see the light of day."

Gray got the clear impression that he was supposed to destroy the files. (Ehrlichman later protested that he couldn't understand how in the world Gray ever got such an idea.) Gray took the files, worried about what he should do with them, hesitated, then finally took them to his home in Connecticut. There, just after Christmas, he burned some holiday trash in the incinerator in his backyard, and he took the documents with him. He had never looked at them before. Just before consigning them to the fire, he took a peek at the top document, saw that it was a phony cable someone had drafted on the Diem assassination—and in horror threw the whole batch of papers into the flames.

At this stage, two-thirds of the cover-up was complete, but the third and vital part—the trail of the money—continued to present problems. One involved Hugh Sloan, Jr., the only official among the whole CREEP crew to display signs of conscience.

Sloan was CREEP's treasurer, and so he had been involved in the dispensing of huge sums of money from the slush fund in CREEP's safe. He was subordinate to Magruder, just as Magruder was subordinate to Stans and Stans to Mitchell. Such was the chain of command. Sloan had become worried about the demands for huge withdrawals of money, and in April he had questioned the $250,000 budget allotted for Liddy's operation. He had asked Stans about it, and Stans had told him, "I don't want to know, and you don't want to know."

Sloan's orders had been to give Liddy what he needed; and in less than two months he had given Liddy $199,000. Then came the Watergate earthquake, and Sloan's life became miserable.

On June 21, Magruder called him in and said that when questioned they would have to agree on the amount of money given Liddy. Magruder suggested that it might be around $75,000 or $80,000. Sloan told him that it was much more than that. Magruder insisted on the lower figure.

"I have no intention of perjuring myself," Sloan told him.

"You may have to," Magruder snapped back.

The next day, FBI agents came to see Sloan at the very time that Fred LaRue was pressuring him about the money problem. LaRue got Sloan away and took him to see Mitchell for "guidance." Mitchell's advice was hardly reassuring. "When the going gets tough, the tough get going," he told the worried Sloan.

When Sloan saw the FBI agents he was relieved to find that they had not come to ask him about money. They wanted to know about Alfred Baldwin, the lookout on the balcony of the Howard Johnson Motel. Sloan had never heard of Baldwin and so could answer truthfully that he knew nothing about him.

But Sloan felt sure that the FBI agents would come back. He began to express his concern to everyone in the administration who, he thought, might be legitimately concerned. Dwight Chapin told him he was overwrought and ought to take a vacation. When Sloan tried to talk to Ehrlichman, Ehrlichman stopped him by saying, "Don't tell me any details. I don't want to know."

On June 23, Stans asked Sloan for an accounting of all receipts and expenditures. This included the record of the Mexican checks, the Dahlberg check, and the Liddy payments. Stans told Sloan to make no copies and to destroy his cashbook. Then Stans destroyed the record Sloan had given him.

The pressure on Sloan was mounting. He finally told Magruder that he would compromise. If the FBI asked him whether Liddy had received $40,000, he would say "Yes." But if he was asked whether Liddy had received more than $40,000, he was also going to say "Yes." Magruder made no comment.

Sloan went once again to Maurice Stans. But all he could get from Stans was the warning that this was a political problem, not the Finance Committee's, and that it was best not to talk about it. Sloan then told LaRue and Stans that he wanted to resign—and did.

Still, at this point everything seemed under control. All records at CREEP had been destroyed, and no one realized that a carbon copy of secret "fat-cat" contributions rested in Rose Mary Woods' files, where it would later be discovered and dubbed "Rose Mary's Baby." The list would show, among other things, how some of the mightiest corporations in America, including Phillips Petroleum, Gulf Oil, and American Airlines, had been muscled to contribute large sums to Nixon's campaign fund, actions that were illegal even before the new April 7 campaign law went into effect, because corporations were already barred from contributing to political campaigns.

Rose Mary's Baby would also show that the dairy industry, which had originally been denied higher price supports, had gotten them after contributing $425,000 to various Nixon campaign committees and that Robert Vesco, the shady international financier accused of looting $224 million from investors, was welcomed at CREEP when he came with $200,000 in hand. Vesco would later be indicted in spite of his "generosity," after the walls of the cover-up had begun to collapse.

Such a collapse, however, seemed unlikely in the summer of 1972. Representative Wright Patman, of Texas, a doughty fighter for the underdog ever since he had openly defied the Ku Klux Klan, posed a brief mini-threat. Patman headed the banking and currency committee of the House, which was sent the GAO report about the $25,000 Dahlberg check, giving Patman the opportunity to call for an investigation. But the administration applied heavy pressure, and Patman's own committee voted him down 20–15 when he asked for subpoena powers. Without such authority to compel witnesses to testify, Patman was helpless—and another threat was averted.

This was the situation on August 29, 1972, when President Nixon held a press conference at his San Clemente estate on the Pacific coast. Dean, who had gone there to report to Haldeman and Ehrlichman on the progress of the cover-up, watched on television as a reporter asked the president whether he didn't think it would be a good idea to name a special prosecutor to investigate the Watergate affair.

The president didn't think so. He said five investigations were already underway, including a "full field" investigation by the FBI. Dean marveled at the president's brazen "hardball" act, but he almost fell off the bed on which he had been reclining at what Nixon said next:

"In addition to that, within our staff, under my direction, the counsel to the president, Mr. Dean, has conducted a complete investigation of all leads which might involve any present members of the White House staff or anybody in government. I can say categorically that his investigation indicates that no one in the White House staff, no one in this administration, presently employed, was involved in this very bizarre incident."

Dean was stunned. There had been, of course, no such thing as a "Dean Report" or a "Dean investigation." The president was telling the American press and public that the very man who was secretly directing the cover-up was, instead, an honest investigator who had found nothing wrong. This was incredible enough, but Nixon did not stop there.

Clark MacGregor, he said, who had succeeded Mitchell as boss of CREEP, was also conducting his own separate investigation. Nixon added that he welcomed all of these investigations because "we want all the facts brought out." And then, in one final, unforgettable line, he added this: "What really hurts in matters of this sort is not the fact that they occur. What really hurts is if you try to cover it up."

CHAPTER 13

THE DANGEROUS MYTH

One of the most dangerous myths about the fall of Richard Nixon is that he was driven from office by a hostile, liberal press. It was a myth that was industriously promoted by Nixon and his aides and one that is still accepted by many of Nixon's die-hard Republican followers.

Actually, of all the techniques used by the White House in the Watergate cover-up, this charge that it was the press, not Nixon, that was at fault is the most insidiously enduring. Yet nothing could be further from the truth.

The real fact is that throughout the 1972 campaign the press behaved more like Nixon's lapdog than his pursuer. The *Washington Post* was the one shining exception. Its vigorous reporting team of Woodward and Bernstein followed the Watergate trail doggedly. *The New York Times,* so often the target of Nixonites, lagged badly. The rest of the American press was even worse.

In the fall of 1972 my literary agent's secretary came back from a European vacation and was astounded at the indifference of the American press and public toward Watergate. "What is happening here?" she asked me. "In London, the papers are full of it, and it is the talk everywhere. Then I come back and find [she gestured helplessly with her hands] practically nothing. Nobody seems to care."

She was right. Ben H. Bagdikian, an expert on the performance of the American press, wrote in the January–February 1973 edition of the *Columbia Journalism Review* that, out of 2,200 reporters stationed in Washington, only fourteen had ever done any substantial work on the Watergate scandal. Television was worse than the press. ABC and CBS had assigned no reporters to Watergate, Bagdikian discovered, and NBC had assigned only one. Contrary to Nixon's contention that he was victimized by a hostile press, Bagdikian said, of the papers that endorsed a candidate, 93 percent endorsed Nixon.

No wonder the American people were poorly informed and indifferent about Watergate. A Gallup poll taken in October, only a few weeks before the election, showed that barely half of the American people had even heard about Watergate and that eight out of ten of those who had, did not see it as any reason to vote against Nixon.

Bagdikian's article was entitled "The Fruits of Agnewism," and in it he theorized that "the Nixon Administration's three-year war against the news media has succeeded. There has been a retrogression in printing newsworthy information that is critical of the Administration and a notable decline in investigation of apparent wrongdoing when it is likely to embarrass the White House."

The three-year war against the news media to which Bagdikian referred had begun in November 1969, when Nixon unleashed his vituperative vice-president, Spiro Agnew. Agnew, who was later to be indicted for taking bribes and forced to resign, roared up and down the country, denouncing "the effete corps of impudent snobs who characterize themselves as intellectuals." He attacked "the tiny and closed fraternity of privileged men, elected by no one," who controlled the media and were, in effect, brainwashing the American people. In the 1970 congressional campaign Nixon joined Agnew on the stump, raising the outcry several decibels higher. He attacked "radiclibs" and "impudent snobs" and "rotten apples." In his election-eve telecast on November 2, he lashed out at "super-hypocrites—those who carry a 'Peace' sign in one hand and who throw a bomb or a brick in another."

It was in such an atmosphere, either cowed or indifferent, that most of the American press would hear of the Watergate grand jury indictments on September 15, 1972. The indictments were limited to the Watergate Seven: Barker, Gonzalez, Martinez, Sturgis, McCord, Hunt, and Liddy. The blame had gone no higher. The White House was ecstatic.

Dean later testified that he received an unusual call to come to the Oval Office. The president greeted him warmly, saying that Haldeman had told him what a fine job Dean had done. Nixon's own tapes show him saying: "Well, you had quite a day today, didn't you? You got Watergate on the way, huh?"

Dean assured him that "not a thing will come crashing down to our surprise" before the election (then just fifty-four days away). Nixon talked about the way his own campaign had been bugged in 1968, then continued: "As you know, a lot of this stuff went on. . . . But the way you, you've handled it—putting your fingers in the dike every time that leaks were sprung here and there . . ."

The talk then turned to the vengeance they would take on their "enemies" once Nixon was reelected. The Internal Revenue Service was going to be put onto Larry O'Brien; the *Washington Post* was going to get its deserts. And Edward Bennett Williams was going to be taken care of.

"I wouldn't want to be on the other side right now, would you?" Nixon asked. "I wouldn't want to be in Edward Bennett Williams' position after this election. . . . I think we're going to fix the [expletive], believe me. We're going to. We've got to, because he's a bad man."

As he was leaving, Dean sounded the only dampening note. "I told him [Nixon]," he later testified, "that there was a long way to go before this matter would end, and I certainly could make no assurances that the day would not come when the matter would start to unravel."

But generally there was euphoria in the White House as the campaign wound down. In the last weeks, George McGovern tried to focus attention on Watergate, but his attacks seemed shrill to most, almost hysterical. And this despite the fact that the *Washington Post* had come up with another exposé. On October 10, 1972, it headlined a Woodward-Bernstein story: "FBI Finds Nixon Aides Sabotage Democrats."

This was the first revelation of a tactic so subversive that it threatened the destruction of the two-party political system. For the first time in American politics, a president had set out to create havoc in the ranks of the opposition party in the primaries. His objective was to destroy by character assassination the strongest Democratic candidates, thus assuring his own reelection. It was a tactic calculated to give the American people only one choice—Nixon.

The supreme importance of this issue was later described by two prominent Democratic senators in vivid terms. Sam Ervin, chairman of the Senate's Watergate committee, said that what the Watergate burglars had been trying to steal "was not the jewels, money, or other property of American citizens, but something more valuable—the most precious heritage, the right to vote in a free election." Majority Leader Mike Mansfield saw the subversion of one party's primary by another as a constitutional issue. "At stake," he wrote, "is the continued vitality of the electoral process in the governmental structure of the nation."

The *Washington Post* got onto the story because Bob Woodward had a male informant highly placed in government circles. Woodward never disclosed his informant's name even to the *Post's* editors. Called "Deep Throat" as a nickname, the informant was outraged at what he saw happening at the highest levels of the Nixon administration and, in secret night meetings with Woodward in basement garages, he kept telling the reporter that things were much worse than anyone knew.

On September 28, Bernstein got a tip from a government lawyer telling him about a campaign of spying and sabotage against the Democrats that had been going on for months. Watergate, he said, was only part of a larger plot.

Bernstein's informant told him to call Alex Shipley, an assistant attorney general in Tennessee. Shipley said that he had known a man named Donald Segretti while both had been attorneys in the army. Shortly before their discharge, Segretti had asked Shipley if he would like to do some political work by joining the campaigns of some of the Democratic hopefuls in order to obtain inside information. For whom, Shipley had asked? For Nixon, Segretti had replied.

"I was really taken aback because all these actions he talked about would have taken place [during] the Democratic primaries," Shipley said.

But, Segretti informed him, this was the purpose; the object was to *disrupt* Democratic campaigns so that all of the stronger candidates would be eliminated. Only McGovern would be left, the man whom Nixon considered the weakest foe.

Woodward, who had taken a weekend off in New York, was summoned back to Washington to see Deep Throat. The FBI had concluded, Deep Throat told Woodward, that the Watergate break-in was only one incident in a far larger campaign of espionage and sabotage. Deep Throat confirmed what the *Post* had been told about Segretti; and he added that Segretti was only one of more than fifty agents employed in the sabotage-the-Democrats campaign.

Before Woodward and Bernstein could write their story, new information practically leaped into their hands. Marilyn Berger, who covered the State Department for the *Post,* told them about a conversation she had had with Ken Clawson, the former *Post* reporter who had become director of communications in the White House. Clawson, she said, told her that he had written the infamous "Canuck" letter that helped to destroy the campaign of the Democratic front-runner, Senator Edmund Muskie of Maine.

It is necessary here to backtrack. Near the end of the bitter 1970 congressional campaign spearheaded by Nixon and Agnew, the Democrats had elected Senator Muskie to speak on nationwide television. Muskie appealed to the voters' senses of reason and decency. His performance contrasted sharply with Nixon's vicious attacks and was generally considered to have helped the Democrats retain control of Congress. The speech made Muskie the favorite for the 1972 Democratic nomination, and public opinion polls in 1971 showed him running well ahead of Nixon.

This was still the situation as New Hampshire primary day approached. The New Hampshire primary has acquired an importance beyond the voting power of the state because it is the first such popular test of a presidential candidate in the nation. On February 24, two weeks before polling day, the Manchester *Union Leader,* whose publisher, William Loeb, was strongly opposed to Muskie, published what became known as the "Canuck" letter.

The letter ostensibly came from a man named Paul Morrison in Deerfield Beach, Florida. It claimed that Muskie, when he was in Florida, had been asked what he knew about blacks. "He didn't have any in Maine, a man with the senator replied. No blacks, but we have Cannocks (sic). What did he mean? we asked. Mr. Muskie laughed and said come to New England and see."

Maine, like other northern New England states, has a sizable number of citizens of French-Canadian descent, but to refer to them as "Canucks" is a racial slur, similar to calling blacks "niggers." Muskie was upset and even further aroused when the *Union Leader* published another letter alleging that Mrs. Muskie had told dirty stories on the campaign trail. Thus on February 26, standing in falling snow on the back of a flatbed truck in front of the *Union Leader* office in Manchester, he attacked Loeb and started to defend his wife. Then, emotionally overwrought, he started to cry. Muskie's campaign was ruined in that moment.

When Marilyn Berger dropped her bombshell, the *Post* went into action. Ben Bradlee, editor of the paper, suggested that Ms. Berger have lunch with Clawson and try to get him to repeat his claim to authorship of the Canuck letter. They dined at Sans Souci, a favorite spot for Washington's elite. Berger told Clawson that Woodward and Bernstein were working on the Canuck story and that she had told them, "Ken said he did it."

"[Clawson] said he wished I hadn't said that," Berger wrote in a memo when she came back. It was not exactly a firm denial. Apparently realizing this, Clawson had then said that he would "deny it on a stack of Bibles."

The *Post* went ahead with the story. Its first paragraph said: "FBI agents have established that the Watergate bugging incident stemmed from a massive campaign of political spying and sabotage conducted on behalf of President Nixon's reelection and directed by officials of the White House and the Committee for the Re-Election of the President. . . .

" 'Intelligence work' is normal during a campaign and is said to be carried on by both political parties. But federal investigators said what they uncovered being done by the Nixon forces is unprecedented in scope and intensity."

This story was only an opening wedge. The *Post* had learned that Segretti had been friendly with a Los Angeles attorney, Lawrence Young. Young, who considered himself a liberal Democrat, said that Segretti had told him many details of his operation. Segretti had told Young that presidential aides had shown him copies of his interviews with the FBI and had briefed him on how to conduct himself before the Watergate grand jury, where he was asked no questions of consequence. Segretti said he had been paid from an account handled by a lawyer who was a high-placed friend of Nixon. And Segretti had told Young that he had had just two contacts in Washington: Dwight

Chapin, the president's appointments secretary, and E. Howard Hunt.

A lot of other details were to come out about the sabotage campaign run by the Nixon forces. Perhaps one of the lowest blows was struck by Segretti and his aides on March 11, three days before the Florida primary. Letters mailed to voters began, "We on the Sen. Ed Muskie staff sincerely hope that you have decided upon Senator Muskie as your choice. However, if you have not made your decision you should be aware of several facts." The "facts" alleged that two of Muskie's rivals, Senator Humphrey and Senator Henry (Scoop) Jackson, had been guilty of a variety of sexual offenses stretching back to 1929. This so-called "black" propaganda that contained not a word of truth effectively smeared both Humphrey and Jackson and demeaned the supposed purveyor of such filth—Muskie.

A whole series of similar feats wrecked the campaigns of every strong Democratic candidate, but nothing that the *Washington Post* said was as explosive as its tying of Dwight Chapin to the scandal. Nixon was especially fond of Chapin, looking upon him almost as a son. Connecting Chapin with the dirty work that had led to Watergate came close to placing the whole scandal in the president's lap for the first time.

The White House reaction, instantaneous and furious, showed that the *Post* had struck a raw nerve. Dean, who had gone to Florida to honeymoon with his new wife, Maureen, was summoned back to Washington. On Sunday, October 15, Dean met in the Roosevelt Room of the White House with Ehrlichman, Chapin, presidential speechwriter Pat Buchanan, Ziegler, and presidential assistant Richard Moore. There they planned a counter-barrage of publicity against the *Post*.

The next day CREEP proclaimed that the *Post* articles were "a collection of absurdities." Maurice Stans said they were "a senseless pack of lies." Clark MacGregor called the *Post's* work "vicious and contemptible." Mitchell, who had stayed in Washington after his resignation from

CREEP, descended to vulgarity and told a *Post* reporter that Mrs. Katharine Graham, the *Post's* publisher, had better watch out.

Ron Ziegler, official spokesman for the president, told reporters, "I will not dignify with comment stories based on hearsay, character assassination, innuendo, and guilt by association." He wanted the White House press corps to know: "We respect the free press. I respect the free press. I don't respect the type of journalism, the shabby journalism, that is being practiced by the *Washington Post.*"

The time would come when Ziegler would apologize for those words, but nothing seemed less likely at the time. The election was in the bag. George Wallace, a potential threat in the South, had been finally eliminated when an assassin's bullet crippled him for life. George McGovern seemed to many too radical. And so Nixon swept to victory in forty-nine of the fifty states, losing only Massachusetts. Few could have imagined that complete exposure and the collapse of his presidency lay just ahead.

An aerial view of the
Watergate hotel-apartment complex
in Washington, D.C.

Above: a disheveled E. Howard Hunt being questioned
by the press after leaving a U.S. district courthouse

Opposite: some of the principal actors in the Watergate drama.
(Top row): John Ehrlichman and Charles Colson;
(middle row): G. Gordon Liddy and Eugenio Martinez;
(bottom row): Felipe DeDiego and Bernard Baker.
All of those pictured here were indicted and sent to prison
for their roles in the Watergate affair.

Former Attorney General
John N. Mitchell

H. R. Haldeman testifying before
the Senate Watergate Committee

Above: Senators Howard Baker and Sam Ervin
confer during some Watergate testimony.
Opposite: James W. McCord shows
the Senate Watergate Committee
how the telephones at the
Democratic National Headquarters were bugged.

Above: John W. Dean III with his wife, Maureen.
Opposite: Special Prosecutor Leon Jaworski
arrives at the Supreme Court to present
arguments that he hopes will force Richard Nixon
to turn over sixty-four White House tapes.

Former President Richard M. Nixon,
seen here after having just resigned the
presidency of the United States. He is about
to board a helicopter that will take him on
the first leg of his journey home to California.
Although Nixon left office as a result
of serious wrongdoings, he still uses the
V-for-Victory gesture in bidding farewell
to his cabinet and staff.

CHAPTER
14
TRIAL OF THE
WATERGATE SEVEN

As 1973 opened, Richard Nixon seemed in supreme command of the American government. He began to move key aides out of the White House into important positions in the various government bureaus and departments, a move represented as necessary to make the government more efficient, but one that was really intended to make every quivering tentacle of the bureaucratic octopus subservient to his will.

Only two minor clouds loomed on the horizon—and behind them a thunderclap that wasn't evident at the time. The first cloud involved the trial of the Watergate Seven, and Nixon had reason to feel that, since the case had been contained at the level of a third-rate burglary, he didn't have to worry about *that*. The second cloud was a scheduled investigation of Watergate by a U.S. Senate committee chaired by Sam Ervin of North Carolina. Though no crusader, Sam Ervin was an expert on the Constitution and a staunch defender of the Bill of Rights, a man to be reckoned with. The hidden thunderclap was to burst in the Senate confirmation hearings of L. Patrick Gray as permanent director of the FBI.

The Watergate trial, with Judge John J. Sirica presiding, came first. Standard operating procedure dictated that this should have been a routine case. In such circumstances, when the evidence is clear, the defendants walk into court, obligingly plead guilty, get bawled out, then receive suspended sentences or slap-on-the-wrist penalties. Case closed.

All outward signs seemed to say that from the administration's standpoint, Sirica would be the ideal judge to try the case. He had been a lifelong conservative Republican and an ardent supporter of Richard Nixon. This author, along with others, expected that he would handle the trial in painless fashion; but in January 1973, while in Washington on a magazine assignment, I received the first hint that Judge Sirica might not follow the script. A lawyer whom I knew, a neighbor and close friend of Sirica, told me, "John is very worried about this case. He's talked to me a little about it, and he's very, very worried about the implications."

My lawyer friend was right. As Judge Sirica later wrote in his book, "I'd have had to be some kind of a moron to believe that no other people were involved. No political campaign committee would turn over so much money to a man like Gordon Liddy without someone higher up in the organization approving the transaction."

In pretrial questioning, Judge Sirica tried to put the prosecutor, Earl Silbert, on the spot. Did Silbert intend to trace the money back to its sources, he demanded? Well, yes, Silbert hoped to do that. What about the $25,000 Dahlberg-Andreas contribution? Well, Silbert hadn't included that in his list of exhibits, but the list wasn't complete yet. What about motive and intent? Silbert said there would be "some evidence." What did he mean by "some evidence"? Silbert wouldn't specify.

The judge thought that he had given Silbert ample

warning, but when Silbert made his opening statement to the jury his recital was confined and bland. He had made no effort to trace the sources of the money. He gave the impression that Liddy had misused the money and gone off on the madcap Watergate adventure on his own. "Liddy was the boss," Silbert said. As for motive, well, the Cubans were poor; they needed money. The facts would suggest, Silbert said, that "it was a financial motive here, financial motive."

Judge Sirica stirred restlessly. "Silbert was now way off the mark," he later wrote. "This was the most limited view of the trial it was possible to take, and it frustrated me."

The trial, which had opened January 8, 1973, now began to run its prescribed course. On January 10, Hunt offered to plead guilty to some counts of the indictment. Judge Sirica insisted that he plead guilty to all eight counts, and on January 11, he did.

The parade began. The four Miamians—Barker, Sturgis, Martinez, and Gonzalez—were so eager to plead guilty that they fired their lawyer, who opposed the pleas, and entered guilty pleas as planned. The newspapers began to charge that the defendants were being paid off by someone to ensure their loyal silence. Judge Sirica questioned the assistant prosecutor, Seymour Glanzer, who told the judge that the newspaper stories contained only "certain innuendoes and insinuations." The prosecutors, he said, had asked the defendants whether they were being paid or coerced to enter guilty pleas, and they had all denied it.

Judge Sirica was more frustrated than ever at the prosecution's willingness to accept such bland denials. He questioned the defendants closely. He demanded that Barker tell him where the $114,000 had come from that had been traced to his bank account in Miami and then back to Liddy. "Your Honor, I got the money in the mail in a blank envelope," Barker said.

"I'm sorry, I don't believe you," Judge Sirica snapped.

The trial continued with only two defendants left—Gordon Liddy and James McCord. When Hugh Sloan testified, Judge Sirica had had more than he could stand. Silbert led Sloan through a bland recital of the money paid out to Liddy. He made no effort, despite the pretrial warning from Judge Sirica, to trace any of the money. The judge called a halt and took over the questioning himself. As he later wrote: "I realized that if I didn't stop it fast, this whole parade would go by, right out of the courthouse, laughing at us. Perhaps some other federal judges would have limited themselves to ruling on objections. But one of the reasons I had always wanted to be a federal judge was that, damn it, nobody could stop me from asking the right questions. I didn't have to sit quietly by and watch this procession."

Under the judge's questioning, Sloan described how he had turned over the Mexican checks to Liddy to be "washed" through the Barker account. Sloan testified that Secretary Stans himself had given him the $25,000 Dahlberg check, which was turned over to Liddy in the same way.

Sloan said he had paid out $199,000 to Liddy. What for? "I have no idea," he said. Who had authorized the payments to Liddy? "Jeb Magruder," Sloan testified.

JUDGE SIRICA: You didn't question Mr. Magruder about the purpose of the $199,000?

SLOAN: No, sir. I verified with Mr. Stans and Mr. Mitchell [that] he was authorized to make those.

JUDGE SIRICA: You verified with who?

SLOAN: Secretary Stans, the finance chairman, and I didn't directly but he verified it with John Mitchell, the campaign chairman.

In this one brief exchange, Judge Sirica had accomplished more than the prosecutors had in all the months they had supposedly been investigating the case. He had broken the

Watergate Seven barrier and traced responsibility to the highest officials in the Nixon reelection campaign—Stans and Mitchell.

It was just the first break in the dike. Soon the whole dam was to give way, and the floodwaters were to come pouring down on the Nixon administration.

On January 30, the jury convicted McCord and Liddy on the Watergate burglary charges. The men were released under bail while probation officers questioned them and examined their backgrounds before making reports to the judge for his consideration in sentencing.

On March 20, as Judge Sirica was walking to his office, he found James McCord standing there. The judge was startled. He had never had any personal contact with defendants prior to sentencing. McCord had a letter he wanted to give the judge. Sirica called in Earl Silbert and U.S. Attorney Harold Titus, Silbert's superior. In their presence he opened and read the letter, then determined to make it public in court the next day. That way, he reasoned, neither the Justice Department nor anyone else could ignore it.

The heart of McCord's letter was in this passage:

"1. There was political pressure applied to the defendants to plead guilty and remain silent.
"2. Perjury occurred during the trial of matters highly material to the very structure, orientation, and impact of the government's case and to the motivation and intent of the defendants.
"3. Others involved in the Watergate operation were not identified during the trial when they could have been by those testifying."

McCord's note said further that his family feared for his life if he talked, and though he personally dismissed such fears, he preferred to talk to the judge privately in chambers. "Since I cannot feel confident in talking with an FBI agent, in testifying before a grand jury whose U.S. Attorneys work for the Department of Justice, or in talking with other government representatives, such a discussion with you would be of assistance to me," McCord wrote.

McCord's bombshell broke the Watergate case wide open. With McCord ready to talk, the elaborate Watergate cover-up was about to be shattered into a thousand pieces.

CHAPTER
15
THE GRAY DEBACLE

L. Patrick Gray, the acting director of the FBI, was a well-meaning man who had instituted some long-needed changes in the Bureau and had had, on the whole, a favorable press. As a result, no one expected any startling disclosures when he came before the Senate Judiciary Committee for confirmation of his appointment on February 28, 1973.

It is obvious from the record that Gray was a man who was subservient to his superiors, so anxious to please that he would carry out orders from higher authority even though he had qualms about them. What wasn't clear until he started to testify was that he was also a bumbler. He didn't know when to leave well enough alone. He didn't know when to stop talking.

The hearings opened on a friendly note, with both senators from Connecticut, Democrat Abraham Ribicoff and Republican Lowell Weicker, vouching for Gray's integrity and ability. The chairman was James Eastland of Mississippi, a Democrat who had been supported by Nixon in his last campaign. There would be no trouble with him. Gray, it seemed, was as good as confirmed.

In his testimony Gray expressed the hope that the Judiciary Committee would not go into Watergate, since the Ervin committee was going to investigate it. Senator Ervin, however, was also a member of the Judiciary Committee, and he had some questions. Taking up a copy of the October 15, 1972, issue of the *Washington Post*—the exposé that had tracked Donald Segretti almost to the door of the Oval Office—Ervin asked Gray about the assertion that a White House aide had shown Segretti copies of his FBI interviews.

Gray was evasive. He would have to check. The FBI, he said, had interviewed Segretti only once, but he personally had never looked into the charge about Segretti's being shown a copy of this interview.

"Then you can't give me any information on that question," Ervin said, apparently ready to drop the issue.

Gray could simply have said, "No, sir, I can't." But he didn't. He kept talking and offered to explain procedures followed in the Watergate investigation. Ervin remarked that showing a witness the results of his FBI interview wouldn't be a likely procedure, would it? "Of course not," Gray replied.

Again, he could have stopped there, but he kept moving ahead, offering "to go into it further if you want me to. . . ."

"Yes, I would like to have that," Ervin said.

Gray kept talking. No one had to prompt him. He disclosed that in mid-July 1972 John Dean had asked him to provide "a letterhead memorandum because he wanted to have what we had to date because the president specifically charged him with looking into any involvement on the part of White House staff members."

Gray said he had forwarded material to Attorney General Kleindienst to be given to Dean. He added: "So you see the possibility there, Senator, and I think what is being driven at is this; the allegation is really being directed toward Mr. Dean having one of these interview reports and showing it to Mr. Segretti."

At this point the entire staff of the *Washington Post*, listening to the confirmation hearings, almost collapsed in shocked surprise. Here was the acting director of the FBI freely giving confirmation of their most sensational charge of the previous October, the one that had brought down upon them the wrath of the White House! Furthermore, Gray was focusing attention for the first time on the role played by Dean. Except for Nixon's mention of the non-existent "Dean Report," Dean had remained a shadowy, virtually unknown figure on the fringes of Watergate. Now Gray was making it clear that he had been a very important actor in the Watergate drama.

Gray said that, "When you are working closely with the office of the presidency, the presumption is one of regularity on the conduct of the nation's business," and it had never occurred to him that anything might be irregular. After the *Post's* story about Segretti, he said, he had asked whether Segretti's political activities should be investigated and "that opinion came back, no."

Senator Robert C. Byrd of West Virginia, then the majority whip and one of the most powerful men in the Senate, asked:

"Were you required to clear the scope of the investigation through the Justice Department?"

"Yes, sir; we work very closely with them on that," Gray responded.

With whom had he worked? Gray's answer was to shake the White House:

"John Wesley Dean, counsel to the president, and I think on maybe half-a-dozen occasions with John Ehrlichman."

John Ehrlichman! The partner of Bob Haldeman in erecting the "Berlin Wall" around the president! Gray was digging the hole deeper and deeper—all the time apparently blind to the disaster he was creating.

Senator Edward M. Kennedy of Massachusetts took up the questioning. Kennedy was better informed than most senators because, as chairman of a judiciary subcommittee, he had conducted his own quiet probe into Watergate after the White House had killed off Wright Patman's attempted investigation. James Flug had handled the inquiry for Kennedy; and it was his information, imparted to Democratic leader Mike Mansfield, that had led to the formation of the Ervin Watergate committee. So Kennedy knew the most sensitive areas. He turned the questioning to the activities of CREEP immediately after the arrest of the Watergate burglars.

Gray confirmed reports that documents in the office of CREEP had been shredded on the morning of the break-in. This was another charge that Nixon spokesmen had tried to dismiss as a newspaper fantasy. But here was the acting director of the FBI saying it was true!

How thoroughly had Segretti been questioned? Had other names cropped up in his questioning? Gray might have said that he didn't know; but, eager as always to oblige, he assured the committee he would go through FBI records and furnish the reports.

He also disclosed that the FBI had wanted to interview Martha Mitchell after her outburst in California, "but Mr. Mitchell said that Mrs. Mitchell's stories and the things that were in the press were not so, and we were not going to interview Mrs. Mitchell. There was no need to interview Mrs. Mitchell, and that was that."

It was obvious that the FBI under Gray had lost a lot of its independence. Its frustrated agents had been blocked time and again by administration requests to Gray. Gray's revelations were so damaging that on March 21 Kleindienst ordered Gray to refuse to answer any more questions about Watergate, but his order came too late. Gray had already testified that he had sent 82 FBI investigative reports to Dean. And on March 22, Gray testified that Dean had "probably lied" to the FBI when he told agents that first time that he didn't know Howard Hunt had an office in the White House.

The disaster wrought by Gray was as complete as it was unexpected. After Gray's disclosures there was virtually no chance of isolating the White House from the Watergate cover-up.

The damage being done by the talkative Gray was recognized by the White House almost at once. On March 6, after another punishing session before the Senate Judiciary Committee, Gray telephoned Ehrlichman. His purpose, clearly, was to make certain that neither Ehrlichman nor Dean would disclose that they had given him those "sensitive" political documents that Gray had burned in his Connecticut incinerator. Ehrlichman recorded the conversation as well as a subsequent one with Dean.

"Been testifying today?" Ehrlichman asked Gray.

"Yeah. I'm having a ball," Gray replied. "I'm being pushed awfully hard in some areas and I'm not giving an inch, and you know those areas and I think you've got to tell John Wesley to stand awful tight in the saddle and be very careful about what he says and to be absolutely certain that he knows in his own mind that he delivered everything he had to the FBI and don't make any distinction between . . . but that he delivered everything he had to the FBI."

"Right," Ehrlichman said.

"And that he delivered it to those agents. . . . This is absolutely imperative."

"All right."

"You know, I've got a couple of areas up there that I'm hitting hard, and I'm just taking them on the attack."

"Okay," said Ehrlichman.

"I wanted you to know that."

"Good. Keep up the good work, my boy. Let me know if I can help."

Ehrlichman then telephoned Dean, telling Dean that Gray had assured him he was " 'hanging firm and very tough.' "

"Yeah, he's really hanging tough," Dean replied sarcastically. "You ought to read the transcript. It just makes me gag."

"Really?" Ehrlichman sounded surprised.

"Oh, it's awful, John."

"Why did he call me? To cover his tracks?"

"Yeah, sure. I laid this on him yesterday," Dean said.

Dean told Ehrlichman that the Judiciary Committee might refuse to confirm Gray until it had questioned members of the White House staff such as himself. Since Nixon had decided to refuse to let his aides testify, this would raise the issue of "executive privilege," and Gray's nomination might be left hanging until that issue was decided in the courts.

Then came perhaps the most chilling, brutally insensitive comment in the whole Watergate scandal.

"Let him hang there?" Ehrlichman wondered. He went on sardonically, "Well, I think we ought to let him hang there. Let him twist slowly, slowly in the wind."

CHAPTER
16
THE IDES OF MARCH

The month of March 1973 was filled with multiple disasters for the Nixon White House. McCord had dropped his bombshell. Gray had incriminated himself to such a degree that he had had to resign as acting FBI director. And the demands for hush-money turned into outright blackmail. The lid was about to blow off the cover-up, littering the landscape with victims.

McCord's letter to Judge Sirica had hardly been read in open court before investigators for the Ervin Watergate committee began to question its author. McCord was willing. A lot of his information was hearsay—that is, he had gotten it from Liddy or Hunt, not firsthand—but McCord had had such close contacts in CREEP that he could give the probers a lot of clues.

One question often raised afterward was, what had made McCord break ranks and talk? The answer may be found in the first profile Bob Woodward did of him right after the break-in. Close friends of McCord had described him as a man of integrity—and one who was intensely loyal. He would faithfully execute any orders issued to him by higher authority. Though retired from the CIA, he was still completely devoted to "The Company," as the agency was called.

It was this ingrained loyalty to the CIA that clashed with the lesser loyalty McCord felt toward CREEP. And when he learned that the Nixon administration was trying to paint Watergate as a CIA crime, McCord went "off the reservation."

The first sign that he was not going to stay in line came during Christmas week, 1972. Jack Caulfield, who had recommended McCord for the post as security director of CREEP, received a letter. It read: "Dear Jack: I am sorry to have to tell you this but the White House is bent on having CIA take the blame for Watergate. If they continue to pursue this course, every tree in the forest will fall and it will be scorched earth. The whole matter is at the precipice right now. Pass the message that if they want it to blow, they are on exactly the right course. I am sorry that you will get hurt in the fallout."

The letter was unsigned, but Caulfield knew that only McCord could have written it. McCord had sensed shortly after the break-in that the White House was trying to off-load responsibility for Watergate on the CIA. Throughout the fall his resentment increased. His stomach churned when he saw pictures in the newspapers of Jeb Magruder and his family. Magruder had been honored by being given the task of stage-managing the second Nixon inaugural; and McCord knew that Magruder was among those responsible for Watergate.

The week before Christmas, McCord's fears that the CIA would be made the scapegoat were confirmed. His lawyer, Gerald Alch, a junior partner of the noted defense attorney F. Lee Bailey, took McCord to lunch at the Monocle Restaurant, one of the plushier luncheon spots on Capitol Hill. Alch suggested to McCord that he should claim Watergate was a CIA operation. McCord protested that he no longer worked for the CIA, but Alch, he says, countered that he could say he had been recalled and CIA records could be doctored since the agency would soon be under "new management" as a result of the Nixon government-wide shake-up. Alch later denied the whole story, but the documented record seems to support McCord. For it was after this luncheon that he wrote letters to an old friend in the CIA, warning of the plot to have the defendants plead guilty and shift responsibility to the CIA.

Three days after the trial began, McCord and Bernard Barker were taken by Alch to see Hunt's attorney, William Bittman. McCord said he understood from Alch that the purpose of the visit was to decide whose word they would accept "regarding a White House offer of clemency." Alch also denied this.

McCord, however, later testified before the Watergate committee that, "I became angered at what seemed to be the arrogance and audacity of another man's lawyer calling in two other lawyers' clients and pitching them for the White House."

After being kept waiting for some time outside Bittman's office, McCord stormed off. Later, he said, Alch told him he would be called the same night "by a friend I had known in the White House."

Here Dean takes up the story. Dean says that Mitchell had heard about McCord's "disagreement" with Alch and asked Dean to have Caulfield contact McCord to see what he planned to do. (Mitchell denied this.) In any event, it is clear that wheels were set in motion.

Dean telephoned Caulfield, who was in California. Caulfield contacted his old friend, Tony Ulasewicz. Ulasewicz telephoned McCord at his home at 12:30 A.M. He said he had a message from Caulfield and McCord should go down Route 355 to a phone booth near the Blue Fountain Inn.

McCord followed instructions, and Ulasewicz read him a message that, he said, had been transmitted from Dean through Caulfield. It was: "Plead guilty. One year is a long time. You will get executive clemency. Your family will be taken care of, and when you get out you will be rehabilitated and a job will be found for you."

McCord replied coolly that he couldn't discuss such matters over the phone. When Ulasewicz called him again the following evening and asked him to meet Caulfield, McCord agreed. He also began to keep a very detailed personal diary.

Caulfield and McCord now had several meetings during which Caulfield tried to get his old friend to follow "the game plan." Caulfield assured McCord at their first meeting that the offer of executive clemency came "from the highest levels" of the White House. Since only the president can grant executive clemency, this implied that the guarantee came from Nixon. But did it? McCord was not convinced.

Dean told Caulfield to go back to McCord and "impress upon him as fully as you can that this offer is a sincere offer which comes from the very highest levels of the White House." Caulfield wanted to be certain just how far he was supposed to go. "I have not used anybody's name with him. Do you want me to?" he asked Dean. "No, I don't want you to do that," Dean told him, "but tell him that this message comes from the very highest levels." Caulfield persisted, "Do you want me to tell him it comes from the president?" Dean replied, "No, don't say that. Say it comes from way up at the top."

Caulfield set up another meeting with McCord at a lonely spot near the George Washington Parkway overlooking the Potomac. According to McCord's later testimony, Caulfield made a hard pitch. He said: "The president's ability to govern is at stake. Another Teapot Dome scandal is possible, and the government may fall. Everybody is on track but you. You are not following the game plan. Get closer to your attorney. You seem to be pursuing your own course of action."

McCord replied that he was going to go his own way. Would he remain silent? "No," McCord said.

As they drove through the Virginia countryside, Caulfield cautioned his friend. It was a chilling piece of advice.

"Jim," he said, "I have worked with these people, and I know them to be as tough-minded as you or I. When you make your statement, don't underestimate them. You know that if the administration gets its back to the wall, it will have to take steps to defend itself."

The violent elimination of McCord, it seemed, might be one of those steps.

McCord told Caulfield, "I have already thought through the risks and will take them when I'm ready. I have had a good life and my will is made out."

In addition to McCord's testimony, there is Dean's account which makes it clear that executive clemency was being considered by the White House. The trouble began not with McCord, but with Hunt's threat to "go off the reservation."

Hunt's wife Dorothy had been killed on December 8 when a United Airlines Boeing 737, in which she was a passenger, crashed into a row of bungalows while attempting to land in dense fog at Chicago's Midway Airport. Only fifteen of the plane's fifty-five passengers survived.

In Mrs. Hunt's recovered handbag investigators discovered $10,000 in $100 bills. What was Mrs. Hunt doing with this amount of money in Chicago? According to a relative, she had been planning to make a down payment on a Holiday Inn franchise.

The death of his wife had Hunt "all bent out of shape." He had four motherless children at home, and right after the first of the year he began to make demands. He wanted to be assured of executive clemency. He tried to get in touch with Chuck Colson, but that canny hatchetman wanted to keep as far away from Watergate as possible. He wouldn't talk to Hunt and he wouldn't talk to Bittman, Hunt's lawyer. The problem, as usual, landed in Dean's lap.

Dean phoned Colson, who protested loudly that he didn't want anything to do with Hunt's demands. Dean went to Erlichman, who decreed that Colson must listen to what Bittman had to say. Dean passed the word to Paul O'Brien, a CREEP lawyer who had been in touch with Bittman, and advised him to tell Bittman to make it quick and to bear down hard before Colson had a chance to shy away.

Bittman did just that. The usually unflappable Colson was in a virtual tizzy when he met with Dean and Ehrlichman after seeing Bittman. "Bittman came at me like a train," he said. Bittman told him that Hunt wanted to plead guilty, but he didn't want Judge Sirica to jail him for years with all those motherless kids he had to take care of. It was clear Hunt wanted a guarantee of executive clemency.

Ehrlichman said he would take it up with the president, but he didn't want Colson to talk to Nixon. He would handle this personally. Ehrlichman's first gambit was to try to get Kleindienst's office to agree to ask the court to go easy on the Watergate Seven. Henry Petersen, who had bent over backward during the summer to accommodate the White House, balked. He told Dean the prosecutors would recommend that Judge Sirica "throw the book" at the defendants.

Blocked in this effort, Ehrlichman had Colson meet with Bittman again. Afterward, Colson was his usual cocky, bouncy self when he reported to Dean and Ehrlichman. He said he had given Bittman "no hard commitment," then added, "I looked at him square in the eye and said, 'You know a year is a long time. And clemency is something that is usually considered around Christmastime here at the White House.'" Bittman, Colson said, got the message. And Hunt would now agree to plead guilty.

As Colson and Dean left Ehrlichman's office, Colson confided that he had violated Ehrlichman's previous order and had talked to the president himself. He had had to feel certain, he said, that he was "on firm ground" when he gave Bittman the pledge he had. Dean felt sick. This direct contact, he knew, put Nixon right into the middle of the illegal cover-up.

The relief that Hunt's clemency problem had been taken care of didn't last for long. After the trial was over, Hunt began to make new demands. The weekend of March 17–18 was a bleak one for John Dean. Hunt demanded he be paid another $120,000 before his sentencing on March 23—or he would talk. Dean could see there was going to be no end to the blackmail.

After Kalmbach had bowed out of the hush-money fund-raising, Fred LaRue had taken over. But fund-raising was becoming more difficult. Everyone knew that the Nixon campaign had ended up practically rolling in $100 bills. Fat cats could hardly be asked to make up a campaign deficit. A kitty of $350,000 had been transferred from CREEP to Haldeman, but this had already been tapped to meet some of the payoff demands. There just wasn't enough money in the till to keep going the hush-money route forever.

And so in desperation Dean telephoned Nixon. He told the president that he had to see him personally to give him the "whole picture" and point out "the soft spots" and possible "problem areas." The president agreed to see Dean for a half-hour the following morning, March 21, 1973.

CHAPTER

17

A CANCER ON
THE PRESIDENCY

A very nervous John Dean walked into the Oval Office for his conference with the president at 10:12 A.M. March 21. Dean felt that the most dangerous problem was not the Watergate burglary itself, but the continuing cover-up through the payment of huge sums of hush-money. He could have quoted Nixon's own words at his August 29, 1972, press conference: "What really hurts in matters of this sort is not the fact that they occur. What really hurts is if you try to cover them up." But naturally no one, least of all the timid John Dean, would have had the nerve to throw the president's words back in his teeth.

After an exchange of pleasantries, Dean launched into a halting explanation, saying he had the impression "you don't know everything I know." Nixon agreed, "That's right."

Dean decided to try to startle the president and focus his attention on the main problem. And so he went directly to the point: "I think there's no doubt about the seriousness of the problem we've got. We have a cancer within—close to the presidency—that's growing. It's growing daily.

... And it basically is because: one, we're being blackmailed; two, people are going to start perjuring themselves . . . to protect other people and the like. And that is just. . . . And there is no assurance."

"That it won't bust," the president said.

The tapes carried the continuing discussion:

DEAN: Now, where, where, are the soft spots on this? Well, first of all, there's the, there's the problem of the continued blackmail—

PRESIDENT: Right.

DEAN: —which will not only go on now, it'll go on when these people are in prison, and it will compound the obstruction of justice situation. It'll cost money. It's dangerous—

PRESIDENT: How much money do you need?

DEAN: I would say these people are going to cost, uh, a million dollars over the next, uh, two years.

PRESIDENT: We could get that.

DEAN: Uh huh.

PRESIDENT: You, on the money, if you need the money, I mean, uh, you could get the money. Let's say—

DEAN: Well, I think we're going—

PRESIDENT: What I mean is you could, you could get a million dollars. And you could get it in cash. I, I know where it could be gotten.

DEAN: Uh huh.

PRESIDENT: I mean it's not easy, but it could be done. But, uh, the question is, who would handle it?

DEAN: That's right. Uh—

PRESIDENT: Any ideas on that?

DEAN: Well, I think that would be something Mitchell might be charged with.

PRESIDENT: I would think so, too.

Later, after Dean's account of this conversation surfaced, Nixon admitted that he had said the million dollars could be raised, "But I said it would be *wrong.*" Haldeman also testified that he had heard the president say "it would be wrong." But the Oval Office tapes gave the lie to both. They showed that Nixon never said, "It would be wrong," and that Haldeman wasn't even present during this part of the discussion.

In fact, instead of the president's expressing any qualms about the payment of hush-money, the whole session was devoted to exploring ways the difficulty might be "managed." At the beginning, when Dean and the president were alone, Dean said that Hunt was threatening to "bring John Ehrlichman down to his knees and put him in jail" if he did not get the $120,000 he was demanding. Hunt had also threatened to sink his old friend, Chuck Colson.

Then the president said, "Don't you, just looking at the immediate problem, don't you have to handle Hunt's financial situation damn soon?" Dean said he had discussed this problem with Mitchell the previous night, and the president said, "After all, you've got to keep the cap on the bottle that much in order to have any options." Dean agreed.

After Haldeman joined the conference, the discussion turned to ways of keeping Haldeman and other White House and CREEP officials from having to testify before the Ervin Watergate committee. One method suggested was to get the Justice Department to impanel a special grand jury. Friends in the department could then guide and control the questioning.

This portion of the March 21 tape was what most horrified the second special Watergate prosecutor, Leon Jaworski, for it showed the president coaching his aides on how to avoid perjury and the charge of obstruction of justice. The idea was for the president to "get out front" by calling for the formation of the grand jury and assuring the public that all of his aides who might be involved would testify before it.

But this presented hazards, too. They discussed the

rules of evidence, with Dean pointing out that a witness could not have a lawyer with him before the grand jury. This followed:

PRESIDENT: Oh, no, that's right.

DEAN: You just can't have a lawyer before the grand jury.

HALDEMAN: Okay, but you do have rules of evidence. You can refuse to talk.

DEAN: You can take the Fifth Amendment.

PRESIDENT: That's right. That's right.

HALDEMAN: You can say you forgot, too, can't you?

PRESIDENT: That's right.

DEAN: But you can't . . . you are in a very risky perjury situation.

PRESIDENT: That's right. Just be damned sure you say I can't remember. I can't recall. I can't give any honest . . . an answer that I can recall. But that's it.

The idea of a new, separate grand jury didn't get very far. The discussion went around and around, but it always came back to Hunt's threat and the blackmail situation that faced them. They all agreed that Hunt had them over a barrel.

PRESIDENT: That's why, for your immediate thing, you've got no choice with Hunt but the hundred and twenty or whatever it is. Would you agree that's a buy-time thing, you better damn well get that done, but fast?

DEAN: I think you ought to be given some signal anyway, to, to—

PRESIDENT: Well, for Christ's sakes get it in a, in a way that, uh—who's going to talk to him? Colson? He's the one who is supposed to know him . . .

There was a second meeting on the afternoon of March 21 with Dean, Haldeman, Ehrlichman, and the president participating. Dean later testified that this meeting "was a tremendous disappointment to me because it was quite clear that the cover-up as far as the White House [was concerned] was going to continue."

Dean was also concerned because Ehrlichman revived the idea of a "Dean Report" that would clear the president. Dean squirmed and dodged to avoid being committed to writing such a false document.

The following morning, March 22, Mitchell, Dean, Ehrlichman, and Haldeman gathered in Haldeman's office. There had been a flurry of phone calls during the night, and Mitchell assured the gathering that Hunt's "problem" had been "taken care of." Everyone knew what that meant—Hunt had been paid off.

The atmosphere in the Oval Office became more relaxed after this. The boys and the president were even able to joke about their need—someone to take all the blame and thus erect a roadblock on the trail that led to the president. There were, understandably, no volunteers.

Dean left the meeting aware that he had failed to make the president see the seriousness of the situation. He was also aware that, since he had warned that they all might be indicted for obstruction of justice, Ehrlichman and Haldeman had considered him, Dean, a new problem.

This was the same day that Gray had testified about Dean lying when first asked about Hunt's White House office. Dean, badly shaken, arose the next morning to read a banner headline across the front page of the *Washington Post:* DEAN PROBABLY LIED. Newspeople and television crews were camped on his doorstep. Dean decided there was nothing he could do except hole up in the house until they went away. Matters grew worse before the day was out, for this was the very day that Judge Sirica would read McCord's letter in open court. Everything was collapsing at once.

Dean, virtually a prisoner in his own house, received a call from the president. Dean told him that he thought McCord could do less damage than Hunt would have done if he had talked. Then the president suggested that Dean and his wife get away from it all and go up to Camp David for a few days. Perhaps while he was there he might find time to write the "Dean Report"?

At Camp David, Dean did a lot of thinking. He knew that the White House desperately wanted a scapegoat—and if he wrote a phony report clearing the White House, he would be that sacrificial goat. The president could say that he hadn't known a thing, that he had been completely deceived by Dean. And so John Dean decided that there would be no "Dean Report."

CHAPTER

18

THE FLOOD
SWEEPS ALL

When Jim McCord broke ranks with his letter to Judge
Sirica, the U.S. Senate was ready to act. At the urging of
Majority Leader Mike Mansfield, the Senate, on February
7, 1973, had passed Resolution Number 60 by a vote of
77 to 0. This resolution established The Select Committee
on Presidential Campaign Activities of 1972, with Sam
Ervin as chairman.

The committee was empowered "to conduct an investigation and study of the extent, if any, to which illegal, im-
proper, or unethical activities were engaged in by any
persons, acting individually or in combination with others,
in the presidential election of 1972 or any campaign, can-
vas, or other activity related to it." Specifically, the committee was instructed to investigate the Watergate break-in
and any possible cover-up.

Ervin selected as the committee's chief counsel Samuel
Dash, a former attorney in the criminal division of the
U.S. Department of Justice and a former district attorney
in Philadelphia. Thus, when Jim McCord spoke out, Dash
hastened to question him.

Though McCord's information was largely hearsay, he had intimate knowledge of the staffing arrangements at CREEP, and he gave Dash the names of subordinates in the office who might confirm some of his story. Following these leads, Dash came to a young woman named Vicky Chern, a secretary who had been responsible for setting up Magruder's meetings. Chern told Dash and his aides that she had kept a duplicate copy of Magruder's appointments in a green diary. She agreed to look for the book, and on April 4 she produced it. It was an important bit of evidence, for it confirmed McCord's account of meetings Magruder had had with John Mitchell.

Vicky Chern told the probers that she had informed Magruder and CREEP counsel Paul O'Brien that she was talking to the committee and had turned over Magruder's appointments book. On hearing this information, Magruder panicked. As he later told the committee, he realized at once that the whole Watergate tale would unravel. Magruder had committed perjury when he testified before the original Watergate grand jury investigating the break-in. He had told the jury that his meetings with Mitchell had had nothing to do with Liddy's espionage schemes. He now met with Mitchell and Dean to make certain that they would support his story.

Dean told him bluntly that he wouldn't. If he was called before the Ervin committee or the grand jury that was reopening the Watergate probe, Dean said, he would refuse to perjure himself. He would tell the truth.

Both Dean and Magruder now realized that the jig was up, and both began to maneuver to make the best deals for themselves that they could. What they wanted above all else was to be granted immunity from prosecution in return for their testimony.

With the Watergate scandal once more erupting in all directions, Assistant U.S. Attorney Silbert, who had cut the first investigation short at the Liddy pass, now suddenly began to make noises like a zealous prosecutor. He subpoenaed Dean to appear before his recalled Watergate grand jury, making Dean the jury's principal witness and instructing him not to talk to anyone else about his testimony. This, in effect, threw a temporary roadblock in the path of the Ervin committee's probe.

Worse, the grand jury now began to leak like a sieve. The newspapers, wearied of Watergate until these most recent developments (even the *Washington Post* had disbanded its Watergate staff), again began to be full of Watergate headlines. Worse still, according to Samuel Dash, every bit of information that Dean gave the grand jury was funneled by Henry Petersen and Attorney General Kleindienst directly to the White House, thus giving Nixon and his aides a chance to prepare answers before witnesses could be questioned by the Watergate committee.

Dean was in a difficult spot. President Nixon was making loud noises about "national security." According to Nixon, virtually everything pertaining to Watergate involved "national security," and this was especially true of the conversations he had had with Dean. These were given the very highest security classification; and if Dean talked, he could be prosecuted.

But Dean and his wily lawyer, Charles Shaffer, found a way around the roadblock. Dean didn't tell the grand jury everything he knew; he held back on actions involving the president. Instead, he wrote down the most vital details, added some documents he had squirreled out of the White House, put everything in a safe-deposit box—and gave Judge Sirica the key. By this maneuver he created a time bomb silently ticking away.

Other bombs were exploding with devastating effect. On April 25, with Daniel Ellsberg's Pentagon Papers trial under way in California, Attorney General Kleindienst learned for the first time about the Liddy-Hunt break-in of the office of Ellsberg's psychiatrist, Dr. Fielding. Kleindienst told the president that Judge W. Matthew Byrne, Jr., who was presiding at the Ellsberg trial, should be informed. Nixon, himself a lawyer, must have known the rules, but he had kept this information (which he had known since March 17, at least) strictly to himself. Pressured by Kleindienst, he reluctantly agreed to inform Judge Byrne of what had happened. The judge, ruling that the whole trial had been tainted by this criminal act of the White House's own agents, then threw out the charges against Ellsberg.

Like one thunderclap following closely upon another, it was disclosed for the first time on April 27 that Patrick Gray had destroyed Hunt's documents at the suggestion of Dean and Ehrlichman. This disclosure brought the chain of criminal actions ever closer to the door of the White House, and Haldeman, Ehrlichman, and Nixon discussed for the first time the possibility that the president might be impeached.

Something had to be done, and on April 30 Nixon acted. He went on nationwide television and told the American people that he had accepted the resignations of Haldeman, Ehrlichman, and Dean. He was also replacing Kleindienst with Elliot Richardson, who had been secretary of defense. Nixon praised Haldeman and Ehrlichman as "two of the finest public servants" he had ever known. He had no such kind words for Dean. In fact, he had hardly finished speaking when FBI agents trooped into Dean's office and sealed off all his files so that he would not be able to document anything he might say.

Nixon's action in wiping out in one stroke the entire high command of his administration created a sensation. It was calculated to show that Nixon was in vigorous command of the situation. He attempted to reinforce this impression by claiming that he had not learned until March 21 (the day of the "cancer on the presidency" talk with Dean) about all the hidden goings-on in his administration. As soon as he learned the facts, he said, he had launched a vigorous investigation to bring out the whole truth. Still acting tough, Nixon made a veiled threat that was almost buried at the time under the more sensational news. No one in his administration, he said, would be granted immunity from prosecution for past illegal acts. This sounded very upright, but it had a hidden meaning that could hardly be lost on potential witnesses—talk and you're going to jail.

While these official pronouncements were capturing the headlines, a secret tug-of-war was apparently going on in an attempt to scuttle the Watergate investigation. According to Samuel Dash, Nixon's agent inside the committee was Senator Howard H. Baker, Jr. (R., Tenn.), the Senate minority leader. Baker had had a secret meeting with Nixon at the White House, and ever afterward, it seemed to Dash, had played a double role—one of conscientious concern in public, wily opposition in secret.

Senator Baker came out of the publicly televised hearings practically wearing a halo. Millions of Americans glued to their television sets admired the way he always seemed to ask important, probing, conscientious questions. Talk started up that he might be presidential material. But insiders in the capital were baffled by what they considered Baker's dual role.

One might expect, of course, that Baker, as the leading Republican spokesman, would defend his party's president as best he could. Still, according to Samuel Dash, if Baker had had his way, the investigation could well have been scuttled at the very beginning.

He began by trying to cut out witnesses. Call just a few on the Watergate break-in and get it over with, he argued; the American people were tired of the whole business. Senator Ervin strongly disagreed. He thought the American people wanted to know the whole truth—and the only way they were ever going to get it was through public hearings conducted by his committee.

This first tactic having failed, Senator Baker tried another. Dash had prepared a witness list that, he felt, would develop the case in an orderly manner so that the public could understand it. Baker prepared another list. Senator Ervin was shocked that Baker's list didn't even have Jim

McCord on it. Baker also wanted to lead off with all of the administration witnesses who would be the targets of any honest investigation—Mitchell, Colson, Haldeman, and Ehrlichman. If Baker's scenario had been adopted, all of these men would have been allowed to give their testimony before any evidence involving them had been developed. There would be no way then to cross-examine them on important issues.

Senator Ervin and the Democratic majority on the committee—joined by Republican Lowell Weicker of Connecticut—scotched this maneuver. Baker's next gambit was to oppose granting immunity to accusing witnesses. When immunity was suggested for Dean, Baker exploded:

"I acknowledge that Dean can be a key witness before this committee. But I believe he is the most culpable and dangerous person in the Watergate affair, and, frankly, I don't want to see him let off the hook."

These actions by Baker forced Dash to resort to an almost unprecedented subterfuge. Since Dean knew of Baker's rendezvous with Nixon in the White House, he did not trust Baker. He and Shaffer, his attorney, said he would talk in private to Dash—and Dash alone. Dean would give Dash the whole story with the understanding that, if he were not given immunity for his testimony before the committee, Dash would forget they had ever met. Dash was to tell no one except Senator Ervin what he had learned. Otherwise, Dean felt certain—and the record certainly supported him—everything he said would be funneled directly back to the White House.

The result was a series of clandestine meetings in Shaffer's law office in Maryland and later at Dean's home. They were long sessions, lasting until 2 or 3 o'clock in the morning, with Dash cross-examining Dean on every point. Dash came away convinced that Dean was a truthful and invaluable witness, and he recommended to the committee that Dean be given "use" immunity—that is, that he could not later be tried for any testimony incriminating himself unless he committed perjury in testifying.

Senator Baker and Senator Edward Gurney (R., Fla.) were outraged. They were incensed at having to vote Dean immunity without knowing what he was going to say. But Senator Ervin, again joined by Weicker, overrode them. The committee voted to grant Dean this limited immunity.

In each of these clashes in executive session, Baker would change his vote after being overridden. Then he would go out with Senator Ervin and appear before the TV cameras, saying that the committee was united, that all members wanted an impartial, thorough investigation.

CHAPTER

19

THE SHOW OPENS

Senator Ervin's Watergate committee opened its nationally televised hearings on May 17, 1973. They were to last for thirty-seven days, and the American public, getting the full story of Watergate for the first time, watched enthralled.

The first hearing merely set the stage, with Sergeant Leeper testifying about how the Watergate arrests were made. The second day saw McCord on the stand, and he placed the Watergate burglary in the lap of John Mitchell. When asked why, after an unblemished career in the FBI and CIA, he had agreed to break into the Watergate and bug Larry O'Brien's phone, McCord said:

"One of the reasons, and a very important reason to me, was the fact that the attorney general himself, Mr. John Mitchell, had his, at his office, had considered and approved the operation, according to Mr. Liddy.

"Secondly, the counsel for the president, Mr. John Dean, had participated in those decisions with him. That was the top legal officer of the United States at the Department of Justice, and the second gentleman the top legal officer at the White House."

McCord then testified in detail about the cover-up "game plan," about the attempt to get him to plead guilty, and about the promises made to him by Jack Caulfield that he would receive executive clemency and "be taken care of." Though there had been rumors in the press, this was the first time McCord's story had been put on the record in detail, and its inescapable implication was that President Nixon himself was involved in the cover-up.

The stage was set for the testimony of two men who could place responsibility for the Watergate crimes at the very top levels of the administration—Jeb Stuart Magruder and John Dean. But before Dash could get these two important witnesses on the stand, he ran into an unexpected roadblock.

The Senate Judiciary Committee had been considering the nomination of Elliot Richardson to succeed Kleindienst as attorney general. Considering Richardson's high reputation, his confirmation hearings would have been routine —except for Watergate.

The Judiciary Committee was concerned about leaving the Watergate prosecution in the hands of a department that had bungled the investigation in 1972 and that would be under the control of the administration being investigated. It demanded that Richardson agree to appoint a special prosecutor, superceding Silbert, Petersen, and the rest of the Justice Department staff. The Judiciary Committee also wanted stiff guidelines that would guarantee the independence of the special prosecutor.

On May 17, the same day the Watergate hearings opened, Richardson agreed. He submitted to the Judiciary Committee an eight-point charter giving the special prosecutor a free hand, and he promised not to "countermand or interfere with" the prosecutor's decisions or to remove him from office "except for extraordinary improprieties."

The man whom Richardson selected was a Harvard professor named Archibald Cox. Cox had served as solicitor general in the Kennedy and Johnson administrations and was highly regarded in legal circles. He agreed to take the job, and the Senate Judiciary Committee, under the impression that it had an ironclad guarantee of the special prosecutor's independence, confirmed the appointments of both Richardson and Cox.

Cox had been Sam Dash's labor law professor at Harvard, and so Dash, who admired Cox, was amazed when he ran into a Cox roadblock. Cox took the position that, since he was on the scene to handle criminal cases arising out of Watergate, there was no need for a Senate investigation. The Watergate probe should end at once without calling Magruder or Dean.

The Nixon administration was delighted. William Safire, who had been a Nixon speechwriter before becoming a columnist for *The New York Times,* and conservative columnist Joseph Alsop took up the cudgels for the White House. Alsop even undertook the dirty job of smearing Dean, calling him a "bottom-dwelling slug."

Dash fought Cox's decision in court and won. This meant that the hearings would continue, and Magruder and Dean would testify.

Magruder came first. He testified on June 14, 1973, about Liddy's wide-ranging plans to wreck the Democrats.

Q. Did there come a time when Mr. Liddy did present his plan to the attorney general, Mr. Mitchell?

A. The first meeting was February 27, I am sorry, January 27, 1971. And we had a meeting in Mr. Mitchell's office.

Q. Who attended that meeting in Mr. Mitchell's office on January 27?

A. Mr. Mitchell, Mr. Dean, Mr. Liddy, and myself.

Q. Could you describe in detail what occurred on January 27 in Mr. Mitchell's office?

A. Mr. Liddy brought with him a series of charts. They were professionally done charts, and had color, some color, on each of the charts. As I recall there were approximately six charts. Each chart contained a subject matter and was headed by a code word. I cannot recall many of the code words, the one I do recall is Gemstone. [The whole budget came to $1 million, Magruder testified.]

Q. Could you give us your best recollection of what some of these projects were?

A. They were, of course, the projects including wiretapping, electronic surveillance, and photography. There were projects relating to the abduction of individuals, particularly members of radical groups that we were concerned about at the convention in San Diego. Mr. Liddy had a plan where the leaders would be abducted and detained in a place like Mexico and that they would then be returned to this country at the end of the convention. He had another plan which would have used women as agents to work with members of the Democratic National Committee at their convention and here in Washington, and hopefully, through their efforts, they would obtain information from them.

Q. With regard to the use of these women as agents, did this involve the use of a yacht in Miami?

A. He envisioned renting a yacht in Miami and having it set up for sound and photographs.

Q. And what would the women be doing at that time?

A. Well, they would have been, I think you could consider them call girls.

Magruder testified that "all three of us were appalled" at Liddy's plan. Not so appalled, however, as to disown it and Liddy. Mitchell merely told Liddy "this was not an acceptable project" and "to come up with a more realistic plan."

A second meeting, with the same four attending, was held in Mitchell's Justice Department office on February 4, Magruder testified. At this meeting, Magruder said, they discussed the possibility of bugging O'Brien's phone and "electronic surveillance at the Fontainbleau Hotel," which was to be the Democrats' headquarters during their convention.

Liddy's ideas were still too grandiose, and this second plan was not approved. But Liddy, Magruder said, was encouraged to keep trying.

After both of these meetings, Magruder testified, he told Gordon Strachan, Haldeman's Man Friday, everything that had happened. Then Chuck Colson got into the act. Magruder testified that Colson "called me one evening and asked in a sense would we get off the stick and get the budget approved for Mr. Liddy's plans."

A third meeting on Liddy's program followed. It was held March 30, 1972, at Key Biscayne. Liddy, Mitchell, Magruder, and Fred LaRue were present. Liddy presented a modified plan with a budget of $250,000, "and Mr. Mitchell agreed to approve the project, and I then notified the parties of Mr. Mitchell's approval."

Magruder added: "It was specifically approved for initial entry into the Democratic National Committee headquarters in Washington, and that at a further date if the funds were available we would consider entry into the presidential contenders' headquarters and also potentially at the Fontainbleau Hotel in Miami."

After the first break-in, Magruder testified, he had transcripts of conversations and photographs of materials found in the Democratic office. He showed these to Mitchell, who was unhappy with the results. Mitchell called in Liddy and told him the information was worthless and not worth what he was being paid for it. Liddy said there had been trouble with one wiretap "and he would correct these matters and hopefully get the information that was requested."

The implication clearly was that Liddy was going to break into the Watergate a second time to fix the faulty bug. And no one objected.

Magruder said that transcripts of the intercepted telephone conversations were typed up by G. Gordon Liddy's secretary, Sally Harmony, and placed in a file marked "Gemstone." Copies were furnished to Gordon Strachan for delivery to Haldeman.

Magruder admitted that he had committed perjury before the Watergate grand jury. He had testified that the first meeting in Mitchell's office (the one that had discussed Liddy's million-dollar fantasy) had been called off and that the second had dealt only with legal problems raised by the new election law.

Q. What role did Mr. Dean play in preparing you for your grand jury appearance?

A. I was briefed by our lawyers and Mr. Mardian. Also, I was interrogated for approximately two hours by Mr. Dean and approximately a half-hour in a general way by Mr. Mitchell.

Magruder was asked what promises had been made to him if he were indicted. He answered:

"They made assurances about income and about being taken care of from the standpoint of my family and a job afterwards and also that there would be a good opportunity for executive clemency. But having worked in the White House. . . . I did not take that as meaning that had a direct relationship with the president at all."

Dean began his testimony on June 25 and was on the witness stand for five days. Except for the documents he had placed in the safe-deposit box for Judge Sirica, he had to rely on his memory because his private files had been sealed off and denied him. Deprived of all check-points, Dean had prepared a 248-page statement from memory. Fortunately for him, he had a photographic mind and a gift for virtually total recall. He testified in a flat, unemotional manner, piling detail upon detail; and he proved an unshakable witness. He realized that he was pitting his word against the word of the president of the United States, who continued to deny all and paint Dean as a liar.

Dean began by drawing a picture of a White House that had become virtually paranoid. Nixon, he said, simply refused to believe that the massive demonstrations against the Vietnam War were not being financed by foreign sources or the Democrats. But the most intensive investigations, Dean said, "never found a scintilla of viable evidence indicating that these demonstrators were part of a master plan." Nixon refused to accept these findings. His attitude was that "the entire system for gathering intelligence was worthless. I was hearing complaints from the president personally as late as March 12 of this year."

One minor incident illustrates Nixon's state of mind. He happened to look out the White House windows in the winter of 1971 "and saw a lone man with a large 10-foot sign stretched out in front of Lafayette Park." This lone demonstrator made the president flip. Dwight Chapin was ordered to get the offender out of the president's sight, and Dean found Chapin about ready to call in some "thugs" to deal with the protestor. Dean blocked the move by summoning the Secret Service, whose agents persuaded the man to move to the other side of the park, where he would be out of presidential eye range.

This was the atmosphere of the White House that had led to the temporary adoption of the Tom Charles Huston plan for domestic intelligence. The Huston plan, labeled Top Secret, was one of the documents that Dean had placed in the safe-deposit box for Judge Sirica. Tom Charles Huston was a young, eager right-winger who had suggested a program so sweeping that it would have violated the rights of virtually every American. Huston called for intensified electronic surveillance of both "domestic security threats" and foreign diplomats; monitoring of American citizens using international communications facilities; increased mail coverage, including the right to open and read anyone's mail; more informants on college campuses; the lifting of restrictions against "surreptitious entry"—in other words, burglary would be sanctioned.

Nixon, as Dean's documents showed, actually approved the plan but soon withdrew his approval as a result of the strenuous objections of FBI Director J. Edgar Hoover.

Hoover did not object to wiretapping and "black bag" jobs when they were conducted by the trained agents of his Bureau; but he was horrified at the idea of fanatic amateurs running amok under the Huston plan. It is perhaps significant that some of the principal elements of the Huston Plan were reborn again in the activities of the Plumbers— with precisely the disastrous results Hoover had feared.

Dean corroborated Magruder's testimony about the first two meetings in Mitchell's office to discuss Liddy's wild plans. After the second session, he said, "I told Haldeman what had been presented by Liddy and told him I thought it was incredible, unnecessary, and unwise. I told him that no one in the White House should have anything to do with this. I said that while the reelection committee needed an ability to deal with demonstrations, it did not need bugging, mugging, prostitutes, and kidnappers. Haldeman agreed and told me I should have no further dealings in the matter."

Dean had supposed that Liddy's program had been abandoned until, on his return from the Philippines, he learned about the Watergate break-in and arrests.

Dean put on the public record for the first time the details of the massive cover-up and his conversations with the president. He revealed that the White House had maintained an "enemies list," and another of the documents he had put in the safe deposit box showed that the constantly expanding list contained literally hundreds of names. The president had instructed Dean to keep track of journalists who were causing "trouble" so that they could be "dealt with" through Internal Revenue Service audits and other forms of harassment. Dean testified that the IRS was induced to hound a reporter from *Newsday*, the big Long Island newspaper, after the paper had run a long and unflattering series about Nixon's close Florida friend, Bebe Rebozo.

Daniel Schorr, the CBS White House correspondent and one of the top journalists in Washington, was on Nixon's enemies list and was subjected to "a full field investigation" by the FBI. When this pressure tactic was revealed, the White House offered the lame explanation—one that evoked derisive laughter—that the FBI had been investigating Schorr because he was being considered for an important government position.

Two other elements in Dean's testimony placed responsibility for criminal acts at Nixon's door. On March 28, Dean said, he had had a long conversation with Egil Krogh, who had headed the Plumbers. He had told Krogh that he felt certain the White House complicity in the break-in of Ellsberg's psychiatrist's office would be traced. Dean explained that Liddy had had a picture taken of himself standing in front of the office. The picture had been taken with a camera borrowed from the CIA—and Liddy had forgotten to take the film out before returning the camera. The CIA had developed the picture and sent copies along to the Justice Department.

Krogh had been stunned at the news of this incredible Keystone Kops caper, but he had said that perhaps it was for the best because he had long been uncomfortable about his role in the burglary. Dean then testified: "I asked him if he had received his authorization to proceed with the burglary from Ehrlichman. Krogh responded no, he did not believe Ehrlichman had been aware of the incident until shortly after it had occurred; rather, he had received his orders right out of the 'Oval Office.' I was so surprised to hear this that I said, 'You must be kidding.' And he repeated again that he had received his instructions from the Oval Office."

Equally damaging to the president was Dean's testimony that Nixon had twice admitted to him that he had promised Howard Hunt clemency. Chuck Colson had told Dean about this promise earlier, but Dean now testified about a meeting with the president on March 15. They discussed the never-ending hush-money demands. Then:

"The president then referred to the fact that Hunt had

been promised executive clemency. He said that he had discussed this matter with Ehrlichman and contrary to instructions that Ehrlichman had given Colson not to talk to the president about it, that Colson had also discussed it with him later. He expressed some annoyance at the fact that Colson had discussed the matter with him."

Dean had begun to talk to the prosecutors on April 2, and he told Haldeman what he was doing. Haldeman told him that he should not talk because "Once the toothpaste is out of the tube, it is going to be very hard to get it back in." This was followed by a strange meeting with the president on April 15, Dean said. The president asked him a number of leading questions, and Dean got the feeling that these were intended to put him on the spot and make the president look good. He began to wonder if the conversation were being taped.

The president said he had been "only joking" when he said a million dollars could be raised for hush-money. Toward the end of the session, the president "got out of his chair, went behind his chair to the corner of the Executive Office Building office, and in a barely audible tone said to me, he was probably foolish to have discussed Hunt's clemency with Colson."

Dean said he had heard a report that the president had a tape on which Dean was recorded as saying that he was seeking immunity in return for testimony against Haldeman and Ehrlichman. Dean was certain that no such discussion had taken place, and he told the committee:

"I do not in fact know if such a tape exists but if it does and has not been tampered with and is a complete transcript of the entire conversation that took place in the president's office, I think that this committee should have that tape because I believe it would corroborate many of the things that this committee has asked me to testify about."

It was a most perceptive suggestion—one that, when acted on, was to result in the downfall of the administration.

CHAPTER
20
THE TAPES

Sam Dash decided to check out Dean's suspicion that the president might have been taping their conversations. He instructed his legal aides to follow this trail when they were questioning minor witnesses. The tactic succeeded in startling fashion on Friday, July 13.

This was the day that Alexander Butterfield came into the interrogation room for routine questioning. So little was anticipated from Butterfield that Dash wasn't even present. The questioning was to be handled by staff aides.

Butterfield's name had come up because he had served in the White House as an aide to Haldeman before being named administrator of the Federal Aviation Agency. Scott Armstrong, one of Dash's assistants, led the way in three hours of questioning.

The White House had put out its own statement about the president's conversations with Dean. Suspiciously, it had followed very closely the sequence of Dean's testimony, with just enough changes in detail to make the president look good; Dean, bad. Armstrong asked Butterfield to examine the statement. How could the conversation have been so completely reconstructed? Butterfield said that it must have been based on more than memory. Then Don Sanders, an assistant minority counsel, blurted out the key question: Could the statement have been composed from a tape?

Butterfield, thinking that the Senate aides knew more than they did, sighed and said in a tone of resignation that not just *one* conversation with the president had been recorded—*all* conversations had been taped.

Sam Dash was almost speechless on hearing the news. Such tapes could corroborate Dean if he were telling the truth—and, in that case, expose the president as a liar! Dash contacted Sam Ervin immediately, and he later quoted the senator as saying: "This is the most remarkable discovery of evidence that I have learned about in my entire experience in the practice of law, as a judge on the bench, and as a United States senator. Why, Sam, this is nothing less than providential . . ."

A subpoena was issued for Butterfield to testify at the next session of the Watergate committee on Monday. In the meantime, Butterfield was having second thoughts. He informed the White House, and he tried to get out of testifying.

He had to go to Russia for treaty negotiations, he said. Why couldn't the committee subpoena someone else? Senator Baker, according to Dash, supported Butterfield and said to Ervin: "You know, Sam, I think Alex is right. Why don't we just excuse him and let him go to Russia to serve his country in the treaty? I think it would be a shame if we did anything to embarrass the government's position with the Soviet Union in this matter just to put Alex on as a witness when, as he says, there are substitute witnesses that can replace him."

Ervin got a stubborn look on his face. No one knew whether or not the White House intended to "stonewall" it and try to prevent other witnesses from testifying. Ervin had Butterfield now, and he wasn't going to let him go.

When Butterfield protested that he might be fired, Ervin argued that this was not likely to happen. It would make the White House look bad if Butterfield were to be dismissed right after he went on national television. (In the end, Butterfield was right. Nixon didn't fire him, but Gerald Ford did as soon as he became president).

It is doubtful that anyone in the television audience who witnessed the Watergate hearings on the afternoon of Monday, July 16, will ever forget it. The scheduled order of witnesses was interrupted because, Dash said, "some very significant information" had to be presented at once. Then Butterfield, a heavyset, roundfaced man, took the stand.

He had been staff secretary at the White House from January 21, 1969 until March 14, 1973. He had reported to Haldeman. In the summer of 1970, he said, he had received an order from the president, transmitted to him through Haldeman and Haldeman's aide, Lawrence Higby, to install listening devices in the White House. A previous system that had been used by Lyndon Johnson had been taken out when he departed. Now President Nixon, Butterfield said, had decided he wanted his conversations taped "to record things for posterity, for the Nixon library."

Butterfield testified that he got in touch with the Technical Security Division of the Secret Service, and their technicians installed a voice-activated system. In other words, no buttons had to be pushed; the tapes began to roll whenever someone started to speak.

The listening devices were placed in the Oval Office, in the president's office in the Executive Office Building (EOB), and in the president's lodge, Aspen Cabin, at Camp David. Telephones everywhere were hooked into the system. The Cabinet Room was bugged with a listening device that had to be manually operated by pressing a button, but the president never bothered to use it.

Q. So far as the Oval Office and the EOB office is concerned, would it be your testimony that the device would pick up any and all conversations no matter where the conversations took place in the room and no matter how soft the conversation may have been?

A. Yes, sir.

Butterfield's testimony made it clear that the truth about Watergate was recorded on a multitude of tapes stored in the White House. It was no longer the word of a minor official, John Dean, against the president of the United States. It was the president versus his own tapes.

The president's men followed Butterfield to the stand. They were full of denials and still arrogant. Most arrogant of all was John Ehrlichman. He argued that the president had inherent power in the name of national security to do anything—and so nothing he had done could be considered illegal. But national security was a vague, all-embracing term. Almost any action a president wanted to take might be justified by saying it was done for national security reasons.

Ehrlichman tried to bolster his argument by citing a 1968 act passed by Congress. This act was actually designed to *outlaw* wiretapping and the disclosure of any information gained from it. Yet Ehrlichman was citing it to justify the president's actions.

Sam Ervin challenged Ehrlichman:

"It says here that this statute, which makes it unlawful to intercept and disclose wire and oral communications shall not interfere with the constitutional powers of the president to—

A. To do anything.

Q.—to do anything necessary to protect the country against five things. The first says actual or potential attacks or other hostile acts of a foreign power. You do not claim that burglarizing Dr. Ellsberg's psychiatrist's office to get his opinion, his recorded opinion, of [the] intellectual or psychological state of his patient is an attack by a foreign power, do you?

This led to a long, involved discussion in which Ervin clearly demonstrated that the act cited by Ehrlichman as the only justification for the president's actions was one designed to protect the privacy of American citizens in their communications. Ervin wound up:

"Well, Mr. Ehrlichman, the Constitution specifies the president's powers to me in the Fourth Amendment. It says; 'The right of people to be secure in their persons, houses, papers, and effects, against unreasonable searches and seizures, shall not be violated, and no warrant shall issue, but upon probable abuse, supported by oath or affirmation, and particularly describing the place to be searched and the person or things to be seized.' Nowhere in this does it say that the president has the right to suspend the Fourth Amendment."

As for the statute Ehrlichman had cited, Ervin declared: ". . . there is not a syllable in there that says the president can suspend the Fourth Amendment or authorize burglary . . ."

Ehrlichman's statement that the president had the right "to do anything" brought him under the fire of Senator Herman Talmadge of Georgia in a half-hour crossexamination.

"Now, if the president," Talmadge asked, "could authorize a covert break-in, and you do not know exactly what that power might be limited [to], you do not think it could include murder or other crimes beyond covert break-ins, do you?"

"I do not know where the line is, Senator," Ehrlichman said. Evidently, he did not rule out even murder.

Talmadge reminded him of a principle of English law that says every man's home, no matter how humble, is his castle, which even the king of England may not enter.

EHRLICHMAN: I am afraid that has been considerably eroded over the years, has it not?

TALMADGE: Down in my country we still think it is a pretty legitimate principle of law. (Applause)

(139)

At the end of this exchange, Senator Ervin summed up what he felt. It was one of the most eloquent passages in the whole Watergate record. He said:

"The concept embodied in the phrase 'every man's home is his castle' represents the realization of one of the most ancient and universal hungers of the human heart. One of the prophets described the mountain of the Lord as being a place where every man might dwell under his own vine and fig tree with none to make him afraid.

"And then this morning Senator Talmadge talked about one of the greatest statements ever made by any statesman, that was William Pitt the Elder, and before this country revolted against the king of England, he said this:

" 'The poorest man in his cottage may bid defiance to all the forces of the crown. It may be frail, its roof may shake, the wind may blow through it, the storm may enter, the rain may enter, but the king of England cannot enter. All his force dares not cross the threshold of the ruined tenements.'

"And yet we are told here today, and yesterday, that what the king of England can't do, the president of the United States can."

It was a moving and poetic speech and a fitting prelude to a months-long battle that would pit the basic principles of democracy against the new authoritarianism that said, in effect, that the president was above the law. And at the very heart of this historic battle were the Nixon tapes.

The Watergate committee wanted them; Special Prosecutor Archibald Cox wanted them. Nixon fought against surrendering them. He argued that "executive privilege" protected the tapes. No president could conduct the affairs of the nation unless he or she could be assured of confidentiality in discussions held with assistants; no president could get honest advice without such assurance. Nixon claimed he was fighting, not to protect himself, but to preserve the ability of all future presidents to govern.

The issue eventually landed in the court of Judge Sirica. Cox argued that he was not engaged in a fishing expedition. He had asked for just nine tapes—those dealing with the conversations of June 20, 1972, three days after the break-in; the September 15 conversation in which Dean said that the president had praised him for containing Watergate; and the later 1973 meetings, especially Dean's March 21 "cancer on the presidency" talk with Nixon.

The president's "executive privilege" contention was weak. There is no mention of executive privilege in the Constitution. On August 29, Judge Sirica signed an order for the president to turn over the tapes for his own inspection. He could then decide whether they contained sensitive or national security matters. If so, these could be deleted and the sections dealing with Watergate could be given to the grand jury for its consideration.

From his home in San Clemente, the president had his press spokesman announce that he would not comply with the order. The president said he would appeal Sirica's ruling to the Court of Appeals. Cox, to Sirica's surprise, appealed also, arguing that the tapes should be given directly to him.

Even as the appeals were under way, the president said he would not surrender the tapes without a "definitive ruling" from the U.S. Supreme Court. In a press conference on September 5, he refused to say what he meant by "definitive," but he left the impression that he would ignore a narrowly divided opinion. In October the Court of Appeals upheld Judge Sirica.

Nixon did not comply. Neither, however, did he make an immediate appeal to the Supreme Court. He had other problems on his mind—and other maneuvers to make.

CHAPTER

21

THE SATURDAY
NIGHT MASSACRE

October 1973 was an unforgettable month for Richard Nixon.

It began with the loss of his vice-president, Spiro Agnew. Agnew, who had been the administration's shrillest voice on the campaign stump, found himself caught in a federal wringer. A federal grand jury sitting in Baltimore charged that Agnew had accepted bribes and kickbacks from contractors while he was county executive of Baltimore County, during his later term as governor of Maryland, and even after he had become vice-president. The jury presented a forty-page bill of particulars, and Elliot Richardson, the new attorney general, told Nixon's new chief of staff, General Alexander Haig, that he had never seen a case with harder facts.

The prospect was horrifying for the administration. Agnew faced either a criminal trial or impeachment proceedings in Congress; and, with Nixon himself threatened with impeachment, the nation confronted a crisis of credibility unlike anything else in its history. After the Civil

War, President Andrew Johnson, who had favored a conciliatory policy toward the South, had been impeached by the Republican radicals in the House of Representatives and had escaped ouster by a single vote in the Senate. This was the only time a president had been impeached—and now there was the very real prospect that both the president and vice-president might have to stand trial for high crimes and misdemeanors.

Clearly, something had to be done to avert this double catastrophe. Elliot Richardson used all of the power of his office to work out a compromise. Finally, on October 10, Agnew yielded to the pressure, the federal prosecutor in Baltimore yielded, and Agnew resigned as vice-president. Then he walked into court and pleaded *nolo contendere*—no contest—to one felony count. He was spared the indignity of spending time in prison and years later would protest his innocence; but the damning charges against him were still on the court record—charges against which he had chosen not to defend himself at the time.

Nixon had to find a replacement to fill the second highest office in the land. He pondered the choice for two days; and then, on the night of October 12, he gathered his Cabinet and the nation's congressional leaders in the East Room of the White House. With television cameras carrying the scene to the nation, Nixon named Representative Gerald R. Ford, the Republican minority leader in the House, to succeed Agnew.

With the Agnew scandal behind him, Nixon next turned his attention to the persistent threat that refused to go away—the tapes. Richardson said later in an affidavit that he met with Nixon after Agnew's plea had been entered and the president had told him, in substance, "Now that we have disposed of that matter, we can go ahead and get rid of Cox."

Days of maneuvering followed. Nixon tried to place himself in a position to justify the action he had already determined to take. He would prepare a transcript of the subpoenaed tapes and have a third-party "verifier" (Senator John Stennis of Mississippi, a Democrat friendly to Nixon) listen to the tapes to compare them with the prepared transcript. Then he would send the transcript to Cox and order Cox to accept it.

If Cox proved stubborn and insisted on getting the actual tapes, then he would be fired. Richardson, informed of the outlines of this plan, warned that he would have to resign if it were fully carried out. Plainly, Richardson said, his honor was at stake because he had promised the Senate in his confirmation hearings that Cox would have a free hand. Richardson felt that he could not renege on this promise given under oath.

Knowing the White House intent, Richardson tried to work out a compromise. But no compromise was possible. Cox, as a conscientious prosecutor, could not accept Nixon's proposal. Who knew what might have been done with the Nixon-prepared transcripts and what might have escaped an aged and hard-of-hearing Senator Stennis? The only real evidence was in the tapes themselves, and no criminal case could be conducted properly without them.

Having greased the skids for Cox, Nixon issued a statement on Friday, October 19. He said he had tried to cooperate with the courts and the Senate; that Senators Ervin and Baker had accepted his Stennis-compromise. (Ervin, at least, seems to have been maneuvered into this, having been summoned to the White House at the last minute and not realizing what was at stake.) After laying this necessary framework, Nixon delivered the presidential crusher: "I have felt it necessary to direct him [Cox], as an employee of the executive branch, to make no further attempts by a judicial process to obtain tapes, notes or memoranda of presidential conversations."

This was the ultimate stonewall. In defiance of the courts, the Senate, and the special prosecutor, Nixon was in effect trying to cut short the Watergate investigation. Cox refused to be hog-tied. He accused the president of "refusing to comply with court decrees," and added: "The instruc-tions are in violation of the promises which the attorney general made to the Senate when his nomination was con-firmed."

The next evening, Saturday, October 20, 1973, will long be remembered as the night of "The Saturday Night Massacre." Nixon ordered Richardson to fire Cox. Richard-son refused—and resigned. Next, General Haig, speaking for Nixon, ordered Deputy Attorney General William Ruckels-haus to do the deed. Ruckelshaus was also unwilling. Haig, the martinet, snapped: "Your commander-in-chief has given you an order. You have no alternative."

Yes he did, Ruckelshaus said. He could resign—and did. But before his resignation could be delivered to the White House, Nixon had fired him. This left Solicitor Gen-eral Robert Bork, a conservative Republican, the next high-est in command. Haig ordered him to get rid of Cox—and Bork did. At 8:22 that Saturday night, Ron Ziegler an-nounced this stunning sequence of events to a shocked and horrified nation.

The backlash was almost instantaneous. Haig later re-called that Saturday as "the night of the firestorm."

The firing of Archibald Cox was probably the worst blunder of Richard Nixon's political life. From that mo-ment, his administration skidded down a steepening slope toward disaster. Typical of the public reaction was the re-mark made by a gas station owner the following Monday morning. "What do I think?" he shrugged. "I think the president got the man before the man could get him."

In Washington, the explosive reaction reminded some observers of the day Pearl Harbor was attacked or President John F. Kennedy was assassinated. Within an hour of Ziegler's statement to the press, lines of cars began to pass the White House with honking horns and signs held up reading HONK FOR IMPEACHMENT. By Tuesday morning, Western Union had processed 150,000 angry telegrams—"the heaviest concentrated volume on record." The number swelled to 220,000 by Wednesday evening; to 430,000 after ten days. One congressman said, "It was as if a dam had broken."

The overwhelmingly hostile reaction presaged the doom of Richard Nixon. Even many who, like Richardson, had felt that the president was innocent, now began to have doubts. Nixon's defiance of the courts, his refusal to give up the tapes, his demand that no more tapes be sought, his firing of the special prosecutor for trying to get the tapes —these did not seem the actions of a man with a clear conscience. Instead, they seemed to be those of a man who had something terrible to hide.

CHAPTER

22

THE TAPE GAP

President Nixon was now under fire from all directions. Judge Sirica, watching on television, saw FBI agents storming and padlocking the special prosecutor's office. It reminded him of "some colonels in a Latin-American country" staging a coup. He thought the firing of Cox was "brutal, contemptible, unjustified, and arrogant."

The nation agreed with him. Eighty-four members of the House introduced bills calling for the president's impeachment. Ninety-eight members backed a bill calling for the creation by Congress of a special prosecutor's office that would be independent of the administration.

The fury of the storm forced Nixon to back down. Just three days after the Saturday Night Massacre, his attorney, Charles Alan Wright, informed Judge Sirica that Nixon would turn over to the court the nine tapes Cox had sought. "This president does not defy the law," Wright said.

Judge Sirica, who had come into court grim-faced and ready to hold the president in contempt if he had to, was relieved that a direct confrontation had been avoided. But he soon discovered that there were some rough seas ahead. There had been no dispute about the existence of all nine subpoenaed tapes, but now Judge Sirica was suddenly informed that two of the tapes had never existed!

Fortunately, this announcement did not take place in a vacuum. Nixon apparently thought that he had gotten rid of the entire special prosecutor's office when he had fired Cox, but he hadn't. Cox's dedicated staff of brilliant young lawyers was left in limbo, but its members stayed on the job and were available to cross-examine witnesses about what had happened to the missing tapes.

Their grilling entangled White House witnesses in a sea of confusion. The lawyers dragged out the admission that Bob Haldeman had been loaned a dozen tapes in July 1973, months after he had been dismissed from office. They also learned that Nixon himself had listened to all of the subpoenaed tapes at Camp David on September 29—more than a month before anyone claimed that two of the tapes were "missing." Why hadn't the court been informed then?

The missing tapes disclosure compounded the disaster of the Saturday Night Massacre for Nixon. *The New York Times,* in a lengthy Sunday editorial, declared: "The one last great service Mr. Nixon can perform is to resign." The *Detroit News* and the *Denver Post,* both Nixon supporters, also called for his resignation. But the most crushing editorial blow was delivered by *Time* magazine. *Time* had supported Nixon in 1960, 1968, and 1972, but now it declared he had "lost his moral authority" and "the confidence of most of the country." It concluded: "The most important decision of Richard Nixon's remarkable career is before him: whether he will give up the presidency rather than do further damage to the country."

Beset on all sides, Nixon decided to forestall congressional action by appointing another special prosecutor of his own. The man he picked was Leon Jaworski, head of one of the largest law firms in Houston, Texas, and a former president of the American Bar Association. A man of the Establishment, Jaworski might have been expected to go easier on the administration than Archibald Cox, the liberal-minded professor from Harvard. Like Judge Sirica, however, Jaworski was devoted to the rule of law, not the rule of men; and he was to prove as relentless in ferreting out the truth as Cox had ever been.

Jaworski was appointed November 1 in the midst of the furor over the missing tapes. This was an issue that had become murkier by the day. General Haig's principal aide in the White House, another military officer, General John C. Bennett, let drop in hearings before Judge Sirica that Rose Mary Woods had complained that she was having trouble with a tape she was transcribing. There was a "gap" on it. Bennett hadn't inquired about the gap, he said.

So Rose Mary Woods was called to the stand. She was questioned by Jill Volner, of the special prosecutor's staff, and the two soon clashed. According to Woods, there was no tape gap. She hadn't been able to find an April 16 tape of a conversation between Dean and the president, but she later learned that this tape hadn't been subpoenaed anyway. And then she found the tape after all. See?

Volner didn't see. She brought out that Woods had struggled for twenty-nine hours to transcribe the first tape given her—that of the crucial June 20, 1972, conversation between Nixon and Haldeman, the first time they had discussed Watergate. What procedures had Woods taken to make certain that no harm came to the original tapes, Volner asked? The questioning went like this:

VOLNER: Were any precautions taken to make sure you would not accidentally hit the erase button?

WOODS: Everybody said be terribly careful. I don't want this to sound like I'm bragging, but I don't believe I am so stupid that they had to go over it and over it. I was told that if you push that button it will erase, and I do know even on a small machine you can dictate over something and that removes it, and I think I used every possible precaution to not do that.

VOLNER: What precautions specifically did you take to avoid . . . recording over it, thereby getting rid of what was already there?

WOODS: What precautions? I used my head. It is the only one I have.

This was a snappish bit of arrogance that would soon return to haunt Rose Mary Woods—and Nixon—when it would be disclosed that Woods was not as efficient as she claimed to be.

An independent panel of experts, some chosen by the White House, some by Jaworski's staff, was now appointed to examine the tapes and make certain that there had been no tampering with them. While this study was pending, President Nixon made one more try, using the PR techniques that he had relied upon so often in the past, to change the color of things. He took to the road in what he called "Operation Candor."

Nixon launched his new PR offensive in the South. In addition to Watergate, his finances had come into question. He had taken a huge tax deduction for filing his vice-presidential papers with the National Archives (a deduction the IRS later determined was illegal), and so had paid less in income taxes than the majority of affluent citizens.

Trying to explain it all in a nationally televised press conference, Nixon declared, "I am not a crook." Even the idea that a president of the United States felt it necessary to make such a declaration caused many to shudder.

Nixon carried on with "Operation Candor." In a tactic similar to when he was going "the PR route" earlier, he tried to make the media the villain. He called the television coverage of the Saturday Night Massacre not just unfair but "outrageous, vicious, and distorted." In Memphis, Tennessee, he met with the conference of Republican governors. Appalled at the damage being done to their party, they asked the president if there were any new "bombshells" hidden in Watergate. He assured them emphatically that there were not.

Less than twenty-four hours later, the worst "bombshell" of the Watergate investigation up to that time exploded in their faces.

Early on the morning of Wednesday, November 21, J. Fred Buzhardt, the lawyer who was now representing Nixon, asked to see Jaworski about an important matter. This turned out to be an 18½-minute gap on the tape of June 20, 1972—the very tape about which Jill Volner had previously questioned Rose Mary Woods.

The shock caused by this revelation can hardly be overemphasized. Haldeman's notes of that June 20 meeting with the president showed that he and Nixon had discussed Watergate, but every syllable of this discussion had been erased from the tape.

Buzhardt pleaded for a few days' delay before making the news public. Jaworski's eyes narrowed and his lips set firmly. He was going to inform Judge Sirica immediately, he said. Sirica at once ordered the White House to turn over all seven reels of June 20 conversations to make certain that nothing else had happened to them. Then he scheduled a public hearing for the following Monday.

Rose Mary Woods returned to the stand. She was no longer the cocky, arrogant witness she had been during her first appearance. She explained that she had been working on the June 20 tape in her White House office on October 1, 1973. While she was typing, she said, her phone rang. As she reached for the phone, she accidentally pressed the "record" button instead of the "stop" button. However, her machine, like many, operated with a foot pedal to stop or start it, thus freeing the secretary's hands for typing. For the machine to have kept running—and erasing—Woods would have had to have kept her foot pressed down on the pedal the whole time she was talking on the telephone.

And why hadn't she revealed this "accident" when she was questioned about this specific tape on November 8? Judge Sirica read her testimony back to her. Woods said she had rushed to tell the president immediately about it, and he had told her not to worry because this wasn't one of the subpoenaed tapes. It was, of course, and perhaps it was even the most vital tape in the whole bunch. But the president's assurance, Woods said, had led her to conclude that her little mistake didn't matter.

The following day, with an identical tape machine plugged in on the witness stand, Jill Volner got Rose Mary Woods to demonstrate just what had happened. The telephone she had answered was almost five feet away, and the demonstration showed that Woods would have had to be a contortionist to reach for the phone with one hand while keeping her extended foot pressed down on the pedal. In fact, she couldn't do it. When she reached for the phone, her foot automatically lifted—and the machine stopped.

"You just picked your foot up off the pedal," Volner informed her.

"That is now because I don't happen to be doing anything," Woods snapped back.

How long had she talked on the phone? No more than four or five minutes. Then how had some 18½ minutes of the tape been erased? Rose Mary Woods, for all her ingenuity, couldn't explain this discrepancy.

After court, the session was adjourned to Rose Mary's White House office. There were the very desk, machine, and telephone that had figured in the gap. White House photographers, perhaps in yet another PR attempt, took color photographs of Rose Mary doing her superhuman stretch. Cartoonists had a field day. They pictured Rose Mary Woods, legs and arms all tangled up, in what they called "Rose Mary Sliding into Third Stretch."

This whole episode called for further probing. General Haig, who had taken Haldeman's place, admitted under questioning by Richard Ben-Veniste of the special prosecutor's staff that he and Nixon had known about the tape gap and the missing tapes before the Stennis compromise had been suggested by Nixon as a substitute for delivering the tapes to the grand jury.

Ben-Veniste wanted to know how Haig could reconcile Rose Mary's 4-to-5-minute "error" with the 18½ -minute gap. Haig incautiously made a remark that was to make headlines and haunt him for days. He speculated that "perhaps some 'sinister force' had come in and applied the other energy source and taken care of the information on that tape." Judge Sirica asked, "Has anyone ever suggested who that sinister force might be?"

Haig's only answer was that women sometimes talked longer on the phone than they thought they did. (Both Dean and Haldeman in their subsequent books indicated their belief that Nixon himself had caused the 18½ -minute gap.)

The gap mystery now landed in the laps of the experts who had been assembled to examine the White House tapes. They worked long and hard, using the most sophisticated equipment in existence. And on January 15, 1974, they issued their report.

It was another shocker. The experts concluded that either Rose Mary Woods was lying or someone, without her knowledge, had deliberately erased the tape. The report was specific. The erasure had been caused by *hand operation,* not by the foot pedal. Magnetic "signatures" on the tape were different if the erasure were caused by hand or pedal. Furthermore, the erasure had been deliberate. The experts detected at least five distinct segments of erasure. In other words, someone who wanted to obliterate what was on that tape had gone over it time and again to make certain it was wiped clean.

These findings by experts of impeccable reputation just about finished what little was left of Nixon's credibility.

CHAPTER
23
INDICTMENTS

There has never been another day in American history quite like March 1, 1974. On that day, the grand jurors who had been studying the Watergate evidence since 1972 returned indictments against seven Nixon aides, including some who had been among the most powerful men in American government.

The three closest Nixon associates—former Attorney General John Mitchell, H. R. Haldeman, and John Ehrlichman—were indicted for obstruction of justice and conspiracy to impede the Watergate investigation. Mitchell and Haldeman were also accused of having given false testimony to the Senate Watergate committee, and Mitchell and Ehrlichman were charged with having lied to the FBI and the grand jury.

Chuck Colson, the one-time hatchetman of the White House, was charged with obstruction of justice and conspiracy. So were Kenneth W. Parkinson, an attorney for CREEP, and Gordon Strachan, the Haldeman aide who had handled the Gemstone bugging transcripts. Strachan was also charged with having lied to the grand jury.

Robert Mardian, the former assistant attorney general who had hunted subversives so relentlessly, was indicted for conspiracy to impede the Watergate investigation.

In addition, the Watergate probe had already produced pleas of guilty from John Dean, Jeb Magruder, and Herbert Kalmbach. Dwight Chapin, the president's appointments secretary, had previously been indicted on two counts of perjury for having given false testimony about the disrupter of Democratic primaries, Donald Segretti. Chapin was later found guilty.

What happened, then, on March 1, was that the criminal justice system had made a clean sweep through the upper echelons of the Nixon administration. Virtually every important official had been charged with a crime, some of a very serious nature.

Now the case went into a new phase, and the focus shifted. The Senate Watergate committee had done its work; it had investigated and exposed. It was now up to the House of Representatives to take action, because only the House could vote to impeach a president. And the House was a virtual cauldron of outrage.

Immediately after the Saturday Night Massacre, so many bills had been introduced in the House for the impeachment of Nixon that the danger existed that impeachment might be voted out of hand, without adequate investigation first. This prospect horrified Representative Carl Albert, the speaker of the house, a careful man who liked to see strict procedures followed. So Albert put Representative Peter Rodino of Newark, New Jersey, chairman of the House Judiciary Committee, in charge of the impeachment inquiry. To head the committee's legal staff, Rodino named John Doar, a Republican attorney with a solid reputation built on his work in the Justice Department during the civil rights battles in the South in the 1960s.

Doar and his staff were helped by the Watergate grand jury that had indicted Nixon's principal aides. The jurors had decided that the evidence they had heard in secret sessions should be passed on to the House committee, and so

they had handed up to Judge Sirica a sealed report sum-
marizing their findings and a bulging brown briefcase
stuffed with tapes and other evidence. On March 26, Judge
Sirica turned this material over to Doar and to the counsel
for the Republican minority on the Judiciary Committee,
Albert Jenner. It was like being given a roadmap that otherwise might have taken Doar and his aides months to puz-
zle out.

Now this infinitely complex case went into another
phase—one that was to overlap with the House Judiciary
Committee's investigation. Special Prosecutor Leon Jaworski, preparing for the trial of the Watergate defendants, decided he needed more White House tapes. The original seven
turned over to Judge Sirica would not be enough. Conversations affecting the roles of the defendants had stretched
out over months, and Jaworski knew that unless he had the
additional tapes, the defendants could contend that discussions proving their innocence were being concealed.

But the minute he asked for more tapes, Jaworski ran
into a new White House stonewall. Nixon refused to yield.
Judge Sirica was amazed at the White House attitude. By
now he had listened time and again to the March 21 "cancer on the presidency" tape. It supported Dean in every respect—and, in effect, convicted the president. Contrary to
his public contention that this was the first time he had
learned what was happening, Nixon had showed no surprise at Dean's revelations; he had agreed he could raise
$1 million for the hush-up; and before the session had ended,
he was saying that Hunt's problem had better be taken
care of "damn quick."

Judge Sirica couldn't imagine that there could be anything much worse on the tapes the White House now insisted on secreting, but the desperation with which Nixon's
attorneys opposed Jaworski's subpoena for sixty-four more
recordings seemed to indicate that there must be something
even more damning on the reels of sequestered tapes.

The House Judiciary Committee was also seeking the
tapes, and congressional sources warned that failure to com-

ply might lead to an immediate vote of impeachment—so a driven Nixon resorted to one last desperate ploy. On April 29, he went on national television and told the American people that he had had prepared complete transcripts of the subpoenaed tapes—and dozens of others. The transcripts, he said, would "at last, once and for all, show that what I knew and what I did with regard to Watergate . . . were just as I have described them to you from the very beginning."

Relying again on public relations to change falsehood into reality, Nixon pointed to a huge stack of loose-leaf notebooks that seemed to stand higher than he did. But the pile of notebooks was phony. The stack had been inflated some five to ten times to make the material Nixon was turning over seem more impressive.

Furthermore, the transcripts were not true transcripts. Judge Sirica, comparing them with the tapes he had listened to, found that the meanings of conversations had been changed; that remarks exposing the president had been deleted. The transcripts were sprinkled with the phrase "expletive deleted" to cover up some of Nixon's more earthy language, and the nation began to laugh about expletives deleted.

Jaworski would not accept the substitute for the real thing, and so he carried his case to the courts. Then came another surprise. In early May, Jaworski disclosed in his brief that the grand jurors, in addition to indicting "the president's men," had also named Richard Nixon as an unindicted co-conspirator. This meant simply that the jurors thought he was just as guilty as the men they had indicted. The only reason they had held back on indicting him was that the Constitution seemed to provide only one method for dealing with a president guilty of "high crimes and misdemeanors"—impeachment.

Judge Sirica upheld Jaworski's demand for the tapes, and Jaworski, catching the White House by surprise, jumped over the intermediate barrier of the Court of Appeals and asked for an immediate decision by the Supreme Court. The chief justice and three other justices on the Court had been appointed by Nixon, and the president had said all along that he would accept only a "definitive ruling." The composition of the Court seemed likely to give him the split decision on which he relied.

But justices, once named to the Court, go their own independent way. On July 24, the Supreme Court upheld Judge Sirica by a unanimous vote of 8–0. (Justice William Rehnquist, having served under Mitchell in the Justice Department, had disqualified himself.) The news of this judicial disaster was carried by telegraphic tickers to San Clemente, where the president was staying. Then the question arose: Who would tell him?

General Haig, ticker copy in hand, went into Nixon's office and broke the news. According to Jaworski's information, "Nixon read it and burst into a tantrum. He reportedly reviled the justices, particularly Chief Justice [Warren] Burger. Haig calmed him." Later, Nixon's newest attorney, James St. Clair, announced that the president would comply with the Court directive.

When the tapes were released, it became obvious why Nixon had fought so stubbornly. The June 23, 1972, tape quickly became known as "the smoking gun." The discussion on that date had dealt with ways to get the CIA to keep the FBI from probing Watergate too deeply. It was clear that everyone recognized there was no real CIA involvement in Watergate, but Nixon sanctioned and directed this particular ploy in the effort to keep the lid on. Yet he had told the nation as recently as May 1974 that he had never intended to use the CIA to shut down the Watergate investigation.

James St. Clair, all the time he had argued the president's case, had not been aware of the contents of this tape. When he learned of it after the Supreme Court decision, he and other White House lawyers were both shocked and scared. They could see the possibility of being named themselves as partners in the cover-up.

As a result, they pressured Nixon to issue a statement along with the release of the tape. In this statement, Nixon admitted that he had approved the attempt to halt the FBI's Watergate investigation. He had not used the CIA maneuver, as he had previously claimed, for "national security" reasons but because he "was aware of the advantages this course of action would have with limiting possible exposure of involvement by persons connected with the reelection committee." Nixon conceded that the new tapes "were at variance with certain of my previous statements."

It was the final exposure. Even Republicans who had been defending Nixon decided they could stand by him no longer. The House Judiciary Committee moved to impeach him. The first of three articles of impeachment charged that Nixon, after the Watergate break-in, "using the powers of his high office, engaged personally and through his subordinates and agents, in a course of conduct or plan designed to delay, impede, and obstruct the investigation of such unlawful entry; to cover up, conceal, and protect those responsible; and to conceal the existence and scope of other unlawful covert activities."

This article spelled out Nixon's misdeeds in nine separate counts. They included condoning the making of false statements to investigators; counseling witnesses to give false testimony; approving the payment of hush-money to silence the Watergate Seven; the attempt to misuse the CIA to halt the FBI investigation into Watergate; disseminating information obtained by investigators to the defendants to aid them in their defense; making false public statements to the American people; holding out the hope of clemency to defendants to keep them silent.

The second article referred largely to the establishment of the Plumbers and their engaging in covert and illegal activities in the attempt to prejudice the rights of a defendant (Daniel Ellsberg) to a fair trial. It also accused Nixon of using the Internal Revenue Service illegally to obtain confidential information and harass citizens with "income tax audits or other income tax investigations . . . in a discriminatory manner."

The third article accused Nixon of an unconstitutional

defiance of House subpoenaes in refusing to turn over the tapes.

On August 20, the full House of Representatives approved the committee report and the articles of impeachment by a vote of 412–3. But by that time Nixon was gone from office.

CHAPTER

24

RESIGNATION

Nixon at first refused to face the inevitable. A gut-fighter in politics, his instinct was to fight on. But "the smoking gun" tape, proving as it did that the president had masterminded the cover-up from the beginning, had disillusioned, disgusted, and enraged even his most ardent supporters. Most felt that they had been betrayed.

Barry Goldwater, one of the staunchest of the band, was handed a copy of the tape transcript and the president's statement as he came off the floor of the Senate. He read them as he walked slowly back to his office in the Senate Office Building. "I was mad," he said later. "I was goddamned mad when I got to the office."

When Nixon had lost even Goldwater, he had lost the whole ball game; but he refused to understand this. In the White House, General Haig wrestled with the infinitely difficult problem of bringing the president to face reality. Haig felt that he was dealing with an unstable personality; he was worried about what the president might do if anyone tried to pressure him. He had to be handled with wily, almost Machiavellian skill.

On August 1, Haig decided that he would have to consult with Vice-President Ford. Convinced that Nixon's resignation was inevitable, Haig wanted to prepare Ford for his own rise to the presidency and to inform him about Nixon's uncertain state of mind. Haig told Ford that he had discussed the seriousness of the new evidence with Nixon, but Nixon had brushed everything off by saying it was "manageable." His was still the old PR attitude; public relations gimmicks could cloak anything.

Haig said that the president had just two options: to ride out the storm or to resign. If he chose the second, he had a number of other options. He could pardon everyone, including *himself,* before he resigned; or he could agree to leave with the understanding that the new president would pardon him. Ford asked Haig about the extent of the president's ability to pardon. "It's my understanding from a White House lawyer," Haig told him, "that a president does have authority to grant a pardon even before criminal action has been taken against an individual."

This conversation took place between Haig and Ford alone. When Ford's chief of staff, Robert Hartmann, and other Ford aides were briefed about it, they were shocked and alarmed. They told Ford that he never should have listened to such a proposal; that, as Hartmann put it, "silence implies consent." And Nixon almost certainly would be notified of this by Haig. Ford then phoned Haig and read a brief statement, saying that he had promised nothing. Haig said he understood.

The ticklish effort to bring the president to see what he had to do without having him erupt in some irrational action continued for days at the White House. Nixon kept insisting that "whatever mistakes I made in handling Watergate . . . the record, in its entirety, does not justify the extreme step of impeachment and removal of a president . . ."

A Cabinet meeting was scheduled for August 6. There was only one question in the minds of all those seated around the Cabinet table: Would the president resign?

They were stunned, therefore, when he opened the meeting by saying:

"I would like to discuss the most important issue confronting the nation and confronting us internationally, too —inflation. Our economic situation could be the major issue in the world today."

He rambled on, finally coming to Watergate. He tried to excuse himself by saying that he hadn't wanted to let "national security matters [get] messed up in this asinine business." What national security matters? He didn't say.

Ford interrupted. He told the president that, if he had known previously what he knew now, "I would not have made a number of the statements I made either as minority leader or as vice-president." Nixon ignored him, talking right on about the economy. George Bush, then chairman of the Republican National Committee, tried to get the discussion back on the Watergate track; this was something that had to be handled quickly, he said. Nixon brushed his remarks aside, talking about the budget and economic strategy.

It remained for crusty William Saxbe, the former senator from Ohio, then attorney general, to put the issue so bluntly that he rocked even Nixon. "Mr. President," he said, "I don't think we ought to have a summit conference [on the economy, as Nixon had suggested]. We ought to be sure you have the ability to govern."

Nixon looked drawn and haggard as the meeting broke up. Secretary of State Henry Kissinger remained with him after the others had gone. Kissinger was too clever to press resignation on the president, but he commented on the attitude of those around the Cabinet table and in a roundabout way hinted that perhaps Nixon should resign.

Nixon held out for one more day. His family, loyal to the end, pleaded with his aides to help in a fight to the finish. But they represented almost the only support he had left. Minority Leader John Rhodes announced in the House that he would vote for impeachment. George Bush wrote the president, urging him to resign. Senator Stennis sent the same message. The final blow was delivered by a delegation of Republican congressional leaders, all of whom recognized that the party could not stand behind the president any longer.

Goldwater headed the delegation, accompanied by Rhodes and Senator Hugh Scott of Pennsylvania, the minority leader in the upper chamber. Before they went in to see the president, Haig told them:

"You must not ask him to resign. He feels that this is a very difficult decision, and he's got to make it himself. He's been up and down several times today. So let him do the talking. But if he asks how many votes he's got, tell him the truth."

Nixon knew that the House was lost; that it would accept the recommendation of Peter Rodino's Judiciary Committee and vote to impeach him. But what chance did he have if he went to trial in the Senate? It takes a two-thirds vote of the Senate to impeach a president. Nixon, then, needed thirty-four votes. Did he have them?

"Barry, how does it look?" he asked Goldwater.

"Well, Mr. President," Goldwater said, "I'll give you my best judgment. You haven't got more than twelve people who will stand with you in the Senate. I've got to be frank; I don't know whether I would be one of them."

"Hugh," the president said, turning to Scott, "do you agree with that?"

"You know, Mr. President," Scott replied, "I'm used to counting votes. I would say it's between twelve and fifteen, but I think it looks very bad."

"It looks damn bad," the president agreed. He told them he would make his decision shortly.

The conference with the congressional leaders tipped the scales. Nixon announced his decision in a televised address Thursday evening, August 8, 1974. He spoke alone from the Oval Office. His eyes were puffy, his jaws sagged.

"Good evening," he began. He recited the difficult decisions that had to be made by a president. Then:

"I would have preferred to carry through to the finish, whatever the personal agony it would have involved, and my family unanimously urged me to do so.

"But the interest of the nation must always come before any personal considerations. From the discussions I have had with congressional and other leaders, I might not have the support of Congress that I would consider necessary to back the very difficult decisions and carry out the duties of this office in the way the interests of the nation would require. . . .

"Therefore, I shall resign the presidency, effective at noon tomorrow. . . .

"I regret deeply any injuries that may have been done in the course of the events that led to this decision. I would say only that if some of my judgments were wrong—and some *were* wrong—they were made in what I believed at the time to be in the best interest of the nation. . . ."

There was no acknowledgment of the crimes of Watergate or of his part in them. Nixon said farewell, posing as a patriot putting the good of the nation above his personal interests when the record surely shows that, for months, he had been thinking only of his personal interests.

The following day, August 9, after an emotional speech to his staff, Nixon and his family flew to San Clemente. And Gerald Ford took the oath of office as the 38th president of the United States.

CHAPTER 25

THE PARDON

President Ford later wrote in his memoirs that he had listened to Nixon's resignation speech "and at the end I was convinced that Nixon was out of touch with reality. The fact that he was linking his resignation to the loss of his congressional base shocked me then and disturbs me still."

President Ford himself may not have been completely in touch with reality. He definitely underestimated the mood of a nation faced with the fact that, for the first time in its history, its most revered political figure—the president of the United States—had been compelled to leave office in disgrace. Most Americans felt a deep sense of anger and betrayal; and so, though Nixon had departed, he remained the most explosive political issue in the nation.

Ford, as he wrote in *A Time to Heal,* had no concept of this when he walked into his first press conference shortly after becoming president. He had hoped to discuss the important issues facing the nation. Instead, he was bombarded with questions about Nixon. Would the former president be prosecuted? Would he be pardoned? What did

Ford intend to do? Taken aback, Ford fumbled and, as he admits himself, gave contradictory answers.

Yet to many the next step should have been obvious. The Watergate burglars had been sentenced. On August 22, Judge Sirica had sentenced John Dean, the invaluable witness, to serve a term of one to four years in prison. So the natural and inevitable question arose: What was the quality of American justice? Was there one law for the lowly, another for the highly placed? Should those who had thought they were merely carrying out presidential orders be imprisoned—and the man responsible for their plight be allowed to go free?

The answers were not simple. Leon Jaworski, the lawyer of the Establishment who had nevertheless fought the Watergate case so vigorously, had qualms about prosecuting Nixon. The picture of a former president behind prison bars disturbed him. He doubted the American people wanted vengeance to be pursued so far.

There were other problems. Nixon had already, in effect, been found guilty by the House Judiciary Committee. The televised Watergate Senate hearings and the televised Judiciary Committee hearings had carried the story to virtually all Americans. And there was more to come. Nixon's top aides—Mitchell, Haldeman, and Ehrlichman—were still facing trial, and, if they were convicted, there would be more adverse publicity. How could Nixon get a fair trial in such circumstances?

Jaworski polled his staff. Almost to a man, they told him that they thought Nixon should be indicted. Afterward, what? Some felt that he should be prosecuted; others said that he should be indicted and a subtle signal sent to President Ford that he could then be pardoned.

George Frampton, who had served on the Special Prosecutor's Watergate Task Force throughout, wrote a most perceptive memorandum. He argued strongly for the indictment of Nixon, and he summed up the arguments against such action in these words:

"As I understand it, three factors could be advanced to justify a decision not to prosecute: (1) public sentiment that Mr. Nixon has suffered enough and a concomitant feeling that the country must get on to other things, prosecution possibly leading to public divisiveness; (2) some feeling that the president did not initiate or mastermind the cover-up but rather fell or was led into assisting the principal actors; (3) a fear that Mr. Nixon could not receive a fair trial.

"My concern is not so much that the counter-vailing factors supporting prosecution outweigh those listed above, but that history will ultimately find each of the above factors illusory and thus judge harshly reliance upon them."

Frampton drew a picture of the almost inevitable future if Nixon were not prosecuted. He wrote:

> I wonder if ten years from now history will endorse the notion that Mr. Nixon has 'suffered enough.' The powerful men around him have also lost their jobs and been disgraced, but many of them will have lost their liberty and livelihood. Mr. Nixon, on the other hand, will continue to be supported in lavish style with a pension and subsidies at the taxpayers' expense until his death. He may re-enter public life, however morally crippled. The prospect of Mr. Nixon publishing his memoirs (and thereby adding several million dollars to his net worth) should remind us that unlike his aides who were convicted of crimes Mr. Nixon will have the 'last say' about his own role in Watergate if he is not prosecuted. This is why, in my view, it is important (absent a full admission of guilt) to have some definitive resolution of Mr. Nixon's Watergate actions.

President Ford might have done well to reason, as Frampton did, that a "full admission of guilt" should have been the condition of any pardon. But he did not.

After that first disruptive press conference, he began, he says, to seriously consider pardoning Nixon. There was no question in his mind about his legal authority to take such action. The precedent was well established. In one case in 1915, the U.S. Supreme Court had written that such a pardon "carries an imputation of guilt; acceptance, a confession of it."

Jaworski sent Ford a memorandum estimating that it would be fully a year after the pending trials were finished before an indictment could be pressed against Nixon. Assuming Nixon's conviction, there would be endless appeals; and the whole political process of the nation would be in an uproar for years to come over the issue of Nixon. The president felt—maybe rightly so—that the nation's business could not be conducted in such an atmosphere; that the whole Nixon issue had to be put behind us quickly. And a pardon was the only way to do this.

The president began, like Frampton, with the hope that Nixon would at least admit his guilt. Ford's associate, Phil Buchen, told Nixon's lawyer: "Look, I think it's important that there be a statement of true contrition from the former president. The president [Ford] tells me that we can't dictate that statement, but in the interests of both your client and the president, I hope you would persuade your client to develop something that would tell the world, 'Yes, he did it, and he's accepting the pardon because he's guilty.' "

Nixon's attorney agreed that this would be desirable, but he doubted that Nixon would go along with it. He confided that Nixon's "ability to discuss Watergate objectively was almost nonexistent." Though Nixon was in poor health (he was soon to be near death from a flare-up of phlebitis, a blood clot in one leg), he was still playing hardball. Ron Ziegler told Ford's deputies, "Let's get one thing straight immediately. President Nixon is not issuing any statement whatsoever regarding Watergate, whether Jerry Ford pardons him or not."

In the end, Ziegler drafted a statement that admitted

virtually nothing. In this, Nixon said only that "I was wrong in not acting more decisively and more forthrightly in dealing with Watergate . . ." He referred to "the depth of my regret and pain at the anguish my mistakes over Watergate have caused the nation and the presidency . . ." He concluded, "That the way I tried to deal with Watergate was the wrong way is a burden I shall bear for every day of the life that is left to me."

Ford later wrote, "Nixon's statement was inadequate. I'd thought he'd be very receptive to the idea of clearing the decks, but he hadn't been as forthcoming as I had hoped. He didn't admit guilt, and it was a good deal less than a full confession."

Nevertheless, Ford went ahead with his decision to pardon Nixon before the former president could be indicted. He chose probably the worst possible way to do it. He went on national television on Sunday, September 8, at 11 o'clock in the morning—a time when as few people as possible would be watching—and announced that he was pardoning Nixon for any and all crimes he may have committed from January 20, 1969, through August 9, 1974. Ford's stated reasons were the doubt that Nixon could get a fair trial, the years-long legal hassle that would be involved, and the necessity to get the Watergate issue behind us and to get on with the affairs of the nation.

The reaction was swift and furious. The Sunday morning timing of the announcement gave it a sneaky coloration, and charges were soon being made—charges that refused to die—that Ford had pardoned Nixon as the result of a secret deal that had made Ford president.

When Ford flew into Pittsburgh to make a speech Monday morning, he was greeted by demonstrators shouting, "Jail Ford, jail Ford!" A workman standing near the airport fence told reporters, "Oh, it was all fixed. He said to Nixon, 'You give me the job, I'll give you the pardon.'"

If Ford's account is to be believed, there was no such secret deal, although Alexander Haig may have gotten the impression from his private conversation with Ford (the one that so horrified Ford's aides) that the new president would not be adverse to a pardon. Ford acted in an attempt to heal the wounds of the nation over Watergate and so avoid further divisiveness. But he had done so clumsily and without getting from Nixon what he should have insisted on—an admission of guilt and contrition.

As a result, the swift Nixon pardon would dog President Ford throughout his administration, and he himself would later admit that it probably played an important role in causing his defeat by Jimmy Carter in the closely fought 1976 presidential election.

CHAPTER

26

AFTERMATH

The scenario that George Frampton had sketched in his memorandum to Leon Jaworski proved uncannily accurate. Virtually everyone went to prison except Richard Nixon, and the injustice of this weighed heavily on Judge Sirica, who decided to reduce the sentences of the lesser figures caught in the scandal.

The five Miamians arrested at the Watergate each served some fourteen months in jail. Hunt was imprisoned for 31½ months. Liddy, who never showed any remorse, was imprisoned for 52½ months until President Carter commuted his sentence in 1977.

Of the higher-ranking figures, former Attorney General Kleindienst escaped with the lightest penalty. He pleaded guilty to one minor misdemeanor count and was given a suspended sentence. Mitchell, Haldeman, Ehrlichman, and Mardian all went on trial before Judge Sirica, and all were found guilty on a variety of charges on New Year's Day, 1975. (Mardian's conviction was later overturned on appeal.)

After their convictions, Judge Sirica reexamined the plight of those who had been sentenced previously on their pleas of guilty—Dean, Kalmbach, and Magruder. All had cooperated with the government and testified, and on January 2, 1975, Judge Sirica reduced their sentences to the time already served in jail.

He subsequently sentenced Mitchell, Haldeman, and Ehrlichman to terms of not less than thirty months and not more than eight years. Again the specter of the man of San Clemente, living free and making large sums of money, arose to haunt the judge. There seemed little justice in keeping the minions in prison while the big chief remained untouched. And so, in the late fall of 1977, Judge Sirica reduced the sentences of Mitchell, Haldeman, and Ehrlichman to the same term he had originally given Dean—one to four years—and in a short time, all were free.

As for Nixon, after recovering from his life-threatening bout with phlebitis, he lived in the imperial manner that Frampton had predicted. His estate at San Clemente was staffed at the taxpayers' expense; and cushioned against financial disaster, Nixon negotiated a contract with Warner Books for a $2 million advance for his memoirs.

He continued to cash in. David Frost, one of television's more noted interrogators, persuaded Nixon to give a series of interviews on his presidency. The deal guaranteed Nixon another $600,000 plus 20 percent of any profits that might be derived from four 90-minute shows. There was suspicion at the time that this would be a "fixed" performance. Otherwise, why should Nixon have agreed to it, even for the money? But Frost insisted on complete editorial freedom, and the television series that resulted came as close as possible to putting Nixon on the witness stand under stiff cross-examination.

In preparation for the series, Frost's team researched Watergate intensely and discovered entirely new material. James Reston, Jr., the professor son of *The New York Times* columnist, was one of Frost's researchers, and he listened to tapes that had previously been ignored.

One was a June 20, 1972, tape of a conversation between Nixon and Colson. This was just three days after the
Watergate break-in—the same day on which the mysterious
$18\frac{1}{2}$-minute gap appeared in the tape of the Nixon-
Haldeman conversation. Fortunately, Reston discovered,
there was no such gap in the Nixon-Colson tape of the same
day.

Early in the conversation Nixon made this highly
peculiar remark: "If we didn't know better, we would have
thought it was deliberately botched."

Colson followed up, remarking: "Bob is pulling it all
together. Thus far I think we've done the right things to
date."

A little later there was this exchange:

NIXON: Basically, they're all pretty hard-line guys.
COLSON: You mean Hunt?
NIXON: Of course, we're just going to leave this
where it is, with the Cubans . . . at times I just stonewall it."

In conclusion, the president remarked: "We've got to have
lawyers smart enough to have our people delay, avoiding
depositions . . . that's one possibility."

Here was a "smoking gun" tape that preceded by three
days the one that had brought the Nixon administration
down. It showed that Nixon had been aware of the cover-up
from the first day and had been determined to "stonewall"
it.

Nixon had always contended that he hadn't known
about the extent of the cover-up and the dangers it posed
until Dean briefed him on March 21, 1973. Yet Reston
found the tape of another Nixon-Colson conversation
that had taken place more than a month earlier—on February 13, 1973. Nixon remarks: "When I'm speaking about
Watergate, that's the whole point of . . . of the election; this
tremendous investigation rests unless one of the seven begins
to talk; that's the problem."

The tape of another Nixon-Colson conversation the following day was even more of a clincher. Nixon began to talk about his favorite subject, the case against Alger Hiss.

NIXON: Hiss was a traitor. It was a cover-up.
COLSON: Yeah.
NIXON: A cover-up is the main ingredient.
COLSON: That's the problem . . .
NIXON: That's where we gotta cut our losses. *My losses are to be cut. The president's losses gotta be cut on the cover-up deal.* (Emphasis added.)

These conversations had not come to light, Reston found, because Colson had pleaded guilty on the Ellsberg break-in case and other charges against him had been dropped. So they had remained—an entire series of "smoking gun" tapes—until Reston discovered them. Armed with such material, Frost confronted Nixon. His tactic was to approach Nixon gingerly. Too antagonistic an approach, he felt, would get nowhere; but, if he could get Nixon talking, he might be able to steer the interviews to the point where Nixon would want to open up.

As a result, the early sessions were devoted to careful sparring until Nixon and Frost became comfortable with each other. Then Frost rocked Nixon by asking him about the conversations with Colson that Nixon had no idea Frost knew about.

Nixon stumbled and resorted to legalistic hairsplitting. He could never have been convicted of obstructing justice, he argued, because his motive wasn't criminal; his motive had been political containment. Frost knew that motive didn't matter. It was the act that counted; and there could be no doubt that Nixon had put a lid on the FBI investigation of Watergate and had sanctioned hush-money payments.

Demolishing Nixon's statement that he "hadn't known" until Dean told him on March 21—and that, as soon as he had learned what had been going on, he had ordered an investigation—Frost hit the former president with a list of sixteen direct quotes from the March 21 tapes. He bored in like a prosecutor, throwing Nixon's own words in his teeth. Anyone watching the program would not be likely to forget Nixon's face as Frost hammered home point after point. Frost later described it in his own words:

"I had gathered momentum as I went along. Nixon remained guarded, his countenance placid through the first several items. Then his lips quivered. His eyes fluttered like the wings of a moth shot through with electric current. His head lurched backward with each new item. He was a man in pain, a man under the lash, but not yet a man ready to concede defeat."

That concession, though less than complete, was yet to come. As the dialogue continued in their taping sessions, Nixon said at one point:

"I brought myself down. I gave them a sword. And they stuck it in. And they twisted it with relish. And I guess, if I'd been in their position, I'd have done the same thing."

He was approaching the point, Frost thought, where he could be brought, ever so gently, to confront the reality of Watergate. But Nixon had to do it in his own way—in one of those long, rambling monologues in which he frequently indulged. He still refused to admit what the tapes revealed—his complete knowledge of the cover-up before his March 21 talk with Dean. But he finally conceded that he did not act as a president should but more as a defense attorney for his aides. He said:

"I will admit that acting as a lawyer for their defense, I was not prosecuting the case.

"I will admit that during that period, rather than acting primarily in my role as the chief law enforcement officer in the United States of America, or at least with responsibility for law enforcement . . . as the one with the chief responsibility for seeing that the laws of the United States are enforced, that I did not meet that responsibility.

"And, to the extent that I did not meet that responsibility, to the extent that within the law, and *in some cases
going right to the edge of the law,* in trying to advise
Ehrlichman and Haldeman and all the rest as to how
best to present their cases, because I thought they were legally innocent, that I came to the edge.

*"And under the circumstances, I would have to say
that a reasonable person could call that a cover-up."* (Emphasis added.)

Then Nixon again backed off, rambling and trying
to justify himself, emphasizing the turmoil caused by the
Vietnam War protestors. He told about his farewell dinner
at the White House with his closest congressional supporters
on the evening of his resignation speech. And he told how he
had cried and had said he hoped he hadn't let them down.
Then, after taking this circuitous route, he told Frost:

"Well, when I said, 'I just hope I haven't let you
down,' that said it all.

"I had.

"I let down my friends.

"I let down the country.

"I let down our system of government and the dreams
of all those young people that ought to get into government, but think it's all too corrupt.

"Yep, I . . . I, I let the American people down. And I
have to carry that burden with me for the rest of my life."

BIBLIOGRAPHY

The spate of magazine articles and books on the Watergate affair is almost endless. Listed here are only those sources that I found valuable.

Ben-Veniste, Richard, and George Frampton, Jr. *Stonewall: The Real Story of the Watergate Prosecution.* New York: Simon & Schuster, 1977.

Breslin, Jimmy. *How the Good Guys Finally Won.* New York: Viking Press, 1975.

Congressional Quarterly Staff. *Complete Watergate: Chronology of a Crisis.* Vols. 1 and 2. Washington, D.C.: The Congressional Quarterly, 1975.

Dash, Samuel. *Chief Counsel: Inside the Ervin Committee —the Untold Story of Watergate.* New York: Random House, 1976.

Dean, John. *Blind Ambition: The White House Years.* New York: Simon & Schuster, 1976.

Drew, Elizabeth. *Washington Journal: A Diary of the Events of 1973–74.* New York: Random House, 1975.

Ford, Gerald R. *A Time to Heal.* New York: Berkley Books, 1980.

Frost, David. *"I Gave Them a Sword:" Behind the Scenes of the Nixon Interviews.* New York: William Morrow & Company, 1978.

Haldeman, H. R. *The Ends of Power.* New York: A New York Times Book, 1978.

Jaworski, Leon. *The Right and the Power: The Prosecution of Watergate.* New York: Reader's Digest Press, 1976.

London Times Investigative Team. *Watergate: The Full Inside Story.* New York: Ballantine Books, 1973.

Lukas, Anthony. *Nightmare: The Underside of the Nixon Years.* New York: Viking Press, 1976.

Rather, Dan, and Gary Paul Gates. *The Palace Guard.* New York: Warner Books, 1975.

Sirica, John J. *To Set the Record Straight.* New York: W. W. Norton & Co., 1979.

Sussman, Barry. *The Great Cover-up: Nixon and the Scandal of Watergate.* New York: New American Library, 1974.

The Watergate Hearings: Break-in and Cover-up. New York: A New York Times Book. Bantam Books, 1973.

White, Theodore H. *Breach of Faith: The Fall of Richard Nixon.* New York: Atheneum Publishers and Reader's Digest Press, 1975.

Woodward, Bob, and Carl Bernstein. *All the President's Men.* New York: Simon & Schuster, 1974.

——. *The Final Days.* New York: Simon & Schuster, 1976.

I also suggest reading *The New York Times* from June 18, 1972, on; two additional articles on voting figures can be found in the issues of September 17 and 21, 1980.

Barry Goldwater's final judgment on Richard Nixon is taken from the transcript of his interview with Harry Reasoner on CBS's *60 Minutes,* originally broadcast on March 9, 1980.

INDEX

Kennedy, John F., 4, 30–31, 40, 50, 68
Kissinger, Henry, 36–37, 40, 163
Kleindienst, Richard, 24, 26, 44, 49, 100, 102, 110, 120–121, 126, 172
Krogh, Egil, Jr., 39–40, 133

LaRue, Frederick C., 23–24, 62, 70–71, 111, 129
Leeper, Paul, 9–11, 125
Liddy, G. Gordon, 18–24, 40–46, 51–54, 58, 62–65, 70–71, 94–97, 105, 127–129, 132–133, 182

Magruder, Jeb Stuart, 17–18, 23–24, 30, 43–44, 51, 64, 70–71, 96, 106, 119, 126–132, 155, 173
Mardian, Robert, 23–24, 51–53, 65, 130, 155, 172
Martinez, Eugenio R., 14, 58, 95
McCord, James W., Jr., 14–15, 19–20, 23, 25, 44, 60–61, 96, 98, 105–109, 117–119, 123, 125–126
McGovern, George, 2, 30, 45, 77–78, 82
Mitchell, John N., 8, 16–18, 23–26, 30, 37, 43, 49, 51, 55, 58–65, 70–71, 81, 96–97, 107, 113–116, 119, 123, 125–129, 154, 167, 172–173
Mitchell, Martha, 60–63, 102

Muskie, Edmund, 79–81

New York Times, The, 2, 11, 36, 39, 74, 127, 148, 173
Nixon, Richard M., 2–7, 16–17, 22, 26–40, 55–56, 74, 76, 81, 93, 110–115, 120–122, 130–134, 140–148, 150, 153, 156–177
    See also Oval office; White House

O'Brien, Lawrence F., 11, 19, 24, 48–49, 76, 125, 128
Oval office, 2, 29–30, 35, 76, 114–115, 133, 137, 164
    See also Nixon, Richard M.; White House

Pentagon Papers, 39–40, 43, 47, 120
Petersen, Henry E., 49, 110, 120, 126

Richardson, Elliot, 121, 126, 142–146

Segretti, Donald, 78, 80–81, 100–102, 155
Select Committee on Presidential Campaign Activities, 118–120, 122
Senate Judiciary Committee, 99–100, 103–104, 126–127
Senate Watergate Committee, 5, 77, 105, 114, 125, 136, 154–155

Silbert, Earl, 49, 94–97, 119–126

Sirica, John J., 4–6, 94–97, 105, 110, 116–117, 120, 130–131, 140–141, 147, 149, 151, 153, 156–158, 167, 172–173

Sloan, Hugh W., Jr., 18, 20, 45, 58, 70–71, 96

Stans, Maurice H., 9, 58, 65–66, 70–71, 81, 96–97

Strachan, Gordon, 45, 50–51, 129, 154

Ulasewicz, Tony, 35–36, 66–67, 107–108

U.S. Justice Department, 24, 26, 35, 49, 58, 97–98, 101, 114, 125–126, 133

U.S. Supreme Court, 37, 40–41, 141, 157–158

Vietnam War, 3, 6–7, 23, 31–32, 36–41, 50, 177

Washington Post, 2, 6, 13, 46–48, 57, 74, 76–77, 80–82, 100–101, 120

Watergate Seven, 64, 76, 93–98, 110

White House, 2–3, 24–26, 37, 40–42, 53–54, 74–77, 81, 100–101, 103–109, 116, 120–121, 135–137
See also Nixon, Richard M.; Oval office

White House tapes, 3, 6, 55, 63–64, 76, 112–115, 134–141, 147–153, 156–159

Wiretapping, 3, 41, 56, 128, 138

Woods, Rose Mary, 9, 71, 149–153

Woodward, Bob, 13–14, 46–48, 57–58, 74, 77–78, 80, 105

Ziegler, Ronald, 22, 29, 43, 48, 81–82, 145, 169